Stoppard

THE PLAYWRIGHT

D0023673

Stoppard

THE PLAYWRIGHT

Michael Billington

METHUEN · LONDON AND NEW YORK

A Methuen Paperback

First published in Great Britain in 1987
in simultaneous hardback and paperback editions
by Methuen London Ltd., 11 New Fetter Lane, London EC4P 4EE
and in the United States of America
by Methuen Inc., 29 West 35th Street, New York, NY 10001.
Copyright © 1987 by Michael Billington

British Library Cataloguing in Publication Data

Billington, Michael
    Stoppard: the playwright.
    1. Stoppard, Tom — Criticism and
    interpretation
    I. Title
    822'.914   PR6069.T6Z/

    ISBN 0-413-45850-4
    ISBN 0-413-45860-1 Pbk

Printed in Great Britain by
St Edmundsbury Press Ltd, Bury St Edmunds, Suffolk

Contents

Illustrations

ROSENCRANTZ AND GUILDENSTERN ARE DEAD: revival directed by Bernard Goss at the Young Vic, London, 1974; left to right: Christoper Timothy (*Guildenstern*), Philip Locke (*Player*), Richard O'Callaghan (*Rosencrantz*). (Photo: Donald Cooper)

THE REAL INSPECTOR HOUND: revival directed by Tom Stoppard for the National Theatre at the Olivier, London, 1985; Roy Kinnear (*Birdboot*, left), Edward Petherbridge (*Moon*, right). (Photo: Donald Cooper)

TRAVESTIES: première production directed by Peter Wood for the RSC at the Aldwych Theatre, London, 1974; John Wood (*Henry Carr*, left), Tom Bell (*James Joyce*, right). (Photo: Donald Cooper)

JUMPERS: première production directed by Peter Wood for the National Theatre at the Old Vic, London, 1974; Michael Hordern (*George Moore*). (Photo: Donald Cooper)

DIRTY LINEN: première production directed by Ed Berman at the Almost Free Theatre, London, 1976; left to right: Richard O'Callaghan (*French*), Malcolm Ingram (*Chamberlain* obscured), Edward de Souza (*Cocklebury-Smythe*), Peter Bowles (*Withenshaw*), Luan Peters (*Maddie*), Benjamin Whitrow (*McTeazle*). (Photo: A. Drago)

NIGHT AND DAY: première production directed by Peter Wood for the RSC at the Aldwych Theatre, London 1974; Diana Rigg (*Ruth Carson*, left), Peter Machin (*Jacob Milne*, right). (Photo: Donald Cooper)

EVERY GOOD BOY DESERVES FAVOUR: revival directed by Trevor Nunn at the Mermaid Theatre, London, 1978; Ian McDiarmid (*Ivanov*). (Photo: Donald Cooper)

CAHOOT'S MACBETH: first London production directed by Ed Berman at the Collegiate Theatre, Bloomsbury, 1979; left to right: Ruth Hunt (*Lady Macbeth*), Peter Woodthorpe (*Inspector*), Stephen D. Newman (*Macbeth*). (Photo: Donald Cooper)

ON THE RAZZLE: première production directed by Peter Wood for the National Theatre at the Lyttleton, London, 1981; Ray Brooks (*Weiberl*, left), Felicity Kendal (*Christopher*, centre), Dinsdale Landen (*Zangler*, right). (Photo: Donald Cooper)

UNDISCOVERED COUNTRY: première production directed by Peter Wood for the National Theatre at the Olivier, London, 1979; Dorothy Tutin (*Genia Hofreiter*, left), John Wood (*Friedrich Hofreiter*, right). (Photo: Donald Cooper)

THE REAL THING: première production directed by Peter Wood at the Strand Theatre, London, 1982; Roger Rees (*Henry*, right), Felicity Kendal (*Annie*, left). (Photo: Donald Cooper)

DALLIANCE: première production directed by Peter Wood for the National Theatre at the Lyttleton, London, 1986; left to right: Sally Dexter (*Mizi*), Tim Curry (*Theodore*), Brenda Blethyn (*Christine*), Stephen Moore (*Fritz*). (Photo: Zoe Dominic)

Chronology of a Career

1937:   Born July 3 in Zlin, Czechoslovakia, the son of
          Eugene Straussler, a doctor employed by Bata, the
          shoe manufacturers.

1939:   Family moved to Singapore.

1942:   Evacuated to India with his mother and brother
          before the Japanese invasion. His father, who
          remained behind, was killed. His mother became
          manageress of a Bata shoe shop in Darjeeling. He
          went to a multiracial English-speaking school.

1946:   Mother married Kenneth Stoppard, who was in the
          British army in India. Family left for England where
          father worked in machine-tool business.

1946–48: Tom at preparatory school in Dolphin,
          Nottinghamshire.

1948–54: At public school, in Pocklington, Yorkshire.

1954–58: Journalist on *Western Daily Press* in Bristol.

1958–60: Journalist on *Bristol Evening World*: news reporter,
          feature writer, theatre and film critic.

1960:   Wrote *A Walk on the Water* – later called *Enter a
          Free Man*. Resigned from his post on *Bristol
          Evening World*.

1963:   Wrote short stories, three of which were bought by
          Faber. Commissioned by publisher Anthony Blond
          to write a novel.

1964:   *The Dissolution of Dominic Boot* and *M is
          for Moon Among Other Things* broadcast on
          BBC Radio. Spent May-October in Berlin on a Ford
          Foundation Grant: wrote *Rosencrantz and
          Guildenstern Meet King Lear*.

1965:   Married Josie Ingle: they had two sons and divorced
          in 1971. Wrote 70 episodes of *A Student's Diary*
          (about an Arab in London) for BBC World Service.

The Gamblers performed at Bristol University.

1966: *If You're Glad I'll Be Frank* on BBC Radio; *A Separate Peace* on BBC TV; co-translation of *Tango* staged by RSC at Aldwych; *Rosencrantz and Guilderstern Are Dead* by Oxford Theatre Group at Edinburgh Festival; *Lord Malquist and Mr Moon* published.

1967: *Rosencrantz and Guildenstern Are Dead* presented by National Theatre at Old Vic; *Teeth* and *Another Moon Called Earth* on TV; *Albert's Bridge* on BBC Radio winning Prix Italia, 1968. Won the John Whiting Award and an Evening Standard Drama Award for *Rosencrantz*.

1968: *Enter a Free Man* and *The Real Inspector Hound* staged in the West End; *Neutral Ground* on Thames TV.

1970: *After Magritte* staged at the Green Banana Restaurant, *Where Are They Now?* on BBC Schools Radio.

1971: *Dogg's Our Pet* staged at Almost Free Theatre.

1972: *Jumpers* staged by National Theatre at Old Vic; *Artist Descending A Staircase* broadcast on BBC Radio. Married Dr Miriam Moore-Robinson, medical director of Syntex Pharmaceuticals and TV personality: they have two sons.

1973: Translation of *The House of Bernarda Alba* performed at Greenwich Theatre. Directed *Born Yesterday* also at Greenwich.

1974: *Travesties* staged by RSC at Aldwych Theatre.

1975: *The Boundary*, co-written with Clive Exton, on BBC TV; adaptation of *Three Men in a Boat* also on BBC TV; first film script, *The Romantic Englishwoman*.

1976: *Dirty Linen* staged at Almost Free Theatre. Spoke in Trafalgar Square for Committee against Psychiatric Abuse. Marched to Soviet Embassy to deliver a petition on dissidents' rights.

1977: Travelled to Moscow and Leningrad with assistant director of Amnesty in Feb., and to Czechoslovakia in June: met dissident playwright Havel. Published four articles on dissidents in these countries. *Every Good Boy Deserves Favour* presented at Royal

Festival Hall; *Professional Foul* on BBC TV.

1978:   *Night and Day* staged at Phoenix Theatre, London. Scripted the film *Despair*.

1979:   *Dogg's Hamlet, Cahoot's Macbeth* toured in Britain and US. Adaptation of Schnitzler's *Undiscovered Country* presented at National's Olivier Theatre.

1980:   Film script of *The Human Factor*.

1981:   Adaptation of Nestroy's *On The Razzle* at National's Lyttelton Theatre.

1982:   *The Real Thing* staged at the Strand Theatre, London. *The Dog It Was That Died* on BBC Radio.

1983:   Translation of Prokofiev's *The Love for Three Oranges* for Glyndebourne Touring Opera.

1984:   *Squaring The Circle* presented on Channel 4; adaptation of Molnar's *Rough Crossing* at National's Lyttelton Theatre.

1985:   Directed *The Real Inspector Hound* at National's Olivier Theatre. Co-scripted the film *Brazil*.

1986:   Adaptation of Schnitzler's *Dalliance* at National's Lyttleton Theatre. Adaptation of Vaclav's Havel's *Large Desolato* at Bristol Old Vic.

1

Introduction

Another book on Tom Stoppard? The shelves are already beginning to groan with exegeses of the work bearing titles like *Tom Stoppard: Comedy as a Moral Matrix* (University of Missouri Press: 1981) that treat the plays as prime sources for academic analysis. Because Stoppard is cerebral, scholarly, allusive and elusive, he tends to attract the professional heavies; and the Americans and the Germans have moved in with a vengeance, publishing essays with titles like 'The Method of Madness: Tom Stoppard's Theatrum Logico-Philosophicum' (*Essays on Contemporary Drama*. Munich: 1981).

My approach is that of a drama critic who views Stoppard's career with a pleasurable bewilderment. He came to the fore in British theatre in 1967 at a time when dramatists were increasingly judged by their political commitment and approximation to social truth, by their willingness to tackle anything from the class system to Vietnam. Stoppard achieved fame with a play, *Rosencrantz and Guildenstern Are Dead*, that was a debonair conceit about two marginal Shakespearean figures waiting for something that would make sense of their lives. And his early works deal with such issues as whether it is better to withdraw stylishly from chaos or engage with life as it is, whether morality is the result of social conditioning or of eternal, God-given laws, whether language itself is a precise instrument or something governed by subjective coloration, whether it is possible to discern design and meaning in the pattern of history or whether one should leave oneself open to random-ness. Stoppard's early plays were philosophical, clever, prankish and funny: a union between the play of ideas and comedy or farce. But it was often hard to tell where he himself stood on any single issue or what lay behind the mask of cleverness.

The obvious thing to say about Stoppard – but none the less true because obvious – is that with time his work has acquired a more tangible sense of political commitment and a greater emotional power. In 1976 he spoke in Trafalgar Square for the Committee against Psychiatric Abuse and marched to the Soviet Embassy to deliver a petition on dissidents' rights. In 1977 he travelled to Czechoslovakia (where he was born in 1937) to meet the playwright Vaclav Havel. He also went to Moscow and Leningrad in the company of the assistant director of Amnesty International. Out of those experiences came a number of articles (including 'Prague: The Story of the Chartists' in the *New York Review of Books*: August 1977), the stage play *Every Good Boy Deserves Favour* and the TV play *Professional Foul*. Stoppard began to engage with public, political issues without sacrificing his wit or legerdemain. He went on to write about press freedom in *Night and Day*, about the self-cancelling absurdities of the espionage game in *The Dog It Was That Died*, about the rise and fall of Solidarity in *Squaring the Circle*. Stoppard became less of an ideological fence-sitter and entered the great arena of public events. The suspicion still lingered that he was wary of writing about private passions or of creating real, three-dimensional characters who wept, suffered or were prey to the daily hurts of mortality. To some extent that accusation was answered by his adaptation of Schnitzler's *Das Weite Land* as *Undiscovered Country* in 1979 which showed the panic, insane preoccupation with honour and profound attraction of death lurking behind the lives of the Austrian bourgeoisie. The watershed was the 1982 play, *The Real Thing* (easily Stoppard's best to date), which combined a good deal of self-criticism with an exploration of pain, love and adultery and a philosophical debate about the relativity of experience including the extent to which things exist outside our perception of them.

Stoppard himself plays down the idea of some lightning conversion from philosophical wordsmith and razzle-dazzle showman to dramatist of political convictions and social purpose. In an interview with *The New York Times* in 1978 he said:

Sixteen years ago, when I first started writing plays, one was surrounded by artists who were making positive statements about social and political questions. But they did not seem to be aware of the difficulties involved in solving those questions. I had a reaction against making heroes for plays who had positive points of view and no qualifications about them . . . But I was always morally, if not politically, involved . . . There was no sudden conversion on the road to Damascus. I know human rights have been around for a long time and I have always been concerned with the daily horrors that I read in the newspapers.

Stoppard points a slightly loaded picture of his fellow-dramatists, many of whom were extremely aware of the difficulties involved in solving political questions: plays like Trevor Griffiths's *The Party*, Howard Brenton's *Weapons of Happiness*, David Hare's *The Great Exhibition* accept a fundamental need for change but are precisely about the impotence of the left in Britain and the futility of many forms of radical protest. Stoppard was not opposed by an army of simple-minded banner-carriers. And, although Stoppard as a private citizen had a long-term concern with human rights and the public world, the real point is that concern only begins to emerge in his work after 1977. There is no Damascene conversion but there is an obvious change of emphasis and a progress towards some kind of declared conviction.

Does it matter? Is an artist any better for confronting the issues of his time? Is Stoppard a more substantial and interesting dramatist for being more visibly committed? Judging by comments he made in a 1973 interview with Janet Watts in *The Guardian*, he would probably say not:

I think that art ought to involve itself in contemporary social and political history as much as anything else but I find it deeply embarrassing when large claims are made for such involvement: when, because art takes notice of something important, it's claimed that art is important. It's not. We are talking about marginalia – the top tiny fraction of the whole edifice. When Auden said his poetry didn't save one Jew from the gas-chamber, he'd said it all. Basically I think that the most committed theatre in the land – I suppose that might be the Royal Court – has got about as much to do with events in the political arena as the Queen's Theatre in Shaftesbury Avenue. I've never felt this – that art is important. That's been my secret guilt. I think it's the secret guilt of most artists.

This raises any number of questions. Of course, Auden was right in the sense that poetry- or any art- does not in an instant affect policy, topple governments or produce action. But art has a depth-charge effect and the history of Western civilization is filled with examples of artists responding directly to public events. The *Lysistrata* of Aristophanes was both about the madness engulfing Greece because of the long drawn-out war with Sparta and about the exclusively male domination of public life. Beethoven's *Eroica* Symphony was written out of a belief that Napoleon represented an incarnation of the spirit of the old Roman consuls (It was only after Napoleon proclaimed himself Emperor in 1804 that Beethoven ripped out the title-page crying 'Is he too no more than a mere mortal? Now he will trample all over the rights of man and indulge only his ambitions'). Picasso's *Guernica* in 1936 was prompted by news of the destruction of German bombers of the Basque town of Guernica and expressed, in powerful terms, the artist's abhorrence of the conflict. Edgar Reitz's 15-hour film *Heimat* (1985) clearly had many sources but one of its intentions was to force Germany to acknowledge its history and to confront the way ordinary people were sucked into the whirlpool of Nazism.

Art has many different motives; and it is true that it does not automatically become important because it deals with important issues. But it is equally true that if art is a response to life, then that response includes events in the public world. And if you took out of world drama all those writers whose plays are fired by a response to public events or the contemporary *Zeitgeist*, you would actually abstract the Greeks, Shakespeare, Schiller, Chekhov, Ibsen, Shaw, Brecht and many more.

Stoppard pursues the argument in more detail in *Travesties* where he presents a number of conflicting notions about the value and purpose of art. But his sympathies seem to lie instinctively with Henry Carr when he says, 'Art is absurdly over-rated by artists which is understandable but what is strange is that it is absurdly over-rated by everyone else.' I find something contradictory in Stoppard's notion of the exaggerated importance attached to art. By what criterion is he judging it? Pure utilitarianism? Clearly art does not feed the hungry, banish evil systems of government, create wealth, topple dictators. What it does do is explain human beings to themselves, tell them what it is like to be other people, inform them about the working of the world, change attitudes and consciousness: all the while providing, one hopes, aesthetic pleasure and the sheer joy of seeing a job well done. If art is unimportant, then it dwindles into a mere leisure-pursuit providing therapy for the unconquerably expressive and a hobby for those with the time and money to enjoy it. If Stoppard really believed art was unimportant, he would not have devoted so much time to writing a TV-drama about Solidarity in *Squaring The Circle* or a commercial play about the freedom of the press in *Night and Day*.

What is true is that the better the art, the more persuasive it is and the greater its effect on human consciousness. Stoppard himself said in a magazine interview in 1976:

> A play is important only if it's good work. I've stopped being defensive about this. I used to feel out on a limb because when I started to write you were a shit if you weren't writing about Vietnam or housing. Now I have no compunction about that. To avert indirectly to *Travesties*, *The Importance of Being Earnest* is important because it says nothing about anything.

Stoppard's opening statement there may be true. But it is art-for-art's sake to go on to claim that Wilde's masterpiece has nothing to say. Like all first-rate work, it is a criticism of life. And, as Eric Bentley has said, it touches on a wide variety of topics including death, money and marriage, the nature of style, ideology and economics, beauty and truth, the psychology of philanthropy, the decline of aristocracy, nineteenth-century moral, the class-system. Wilde's witticisms offer a constant satirical counterpoint to the absurdities of the action; and it is odd that a dramatist who has studied the play so closely cannot see that.

I question some of the assumptions underlying Stoppard's work. He remains, however, a witty, gifted, complex dramatist. He writes about serious issues in a high-spirited way. He makes one want to argue with him. He constantly challenges one's notions of what a play can do. For most of this century the conventional idea of the Ibsenite, well-made play has been under attack: Shaw showed in work like *Getting Married* and *Misalliance* that drama could be built out of disquisitory talk, Pirandello proved that it could be constructed out of a constant conflict between reality and illusion, Beckett demonstrated in

Waiting for Godot that it could be derived from a confrontation with the meaninglessness of existence. Stoppard, formally owes something to all those writers. But the fascination of his work lies in watching his progress from a drama of manipulative cleverness to one that is animated by profound political and moral convictions and that is inhabited by real, breathing, suffering human beings. In the course of this book, I hope to bring out certain recurrent themes, to prove that some of Stoppard's best work has been written for television and radio and to examine his progress to a point where heart and head seem to be operating in true harmony.

2

Young Tom

Stoppard's career as a playwright began in 1960 with a one-act piece, *The Gamblers*, which he once shrugged off to Kenneth Tynan as *'Waiting for Godot* in the death cell – prisoner and jailer – I'm sure you can imagine the rest.' Apart from a single performance by Bristol University students in 1965, the play has sunk into oblivion. His first work performed by professionals was *A Walk on the Water* which had a protracted history. Stoppard wrote it for the stage in 1960, re-wrote it as a 90-minute television play which was transmitted in 1963 and then revised it further as a two-act stage play, *Enter a Free Man*, which was produced in the West End with Michael Hordern in 1968. This play, conceived in 1960 and finally staged eight years later, neatly marks off the first stage of Stoppard's career: his transition from a Bristol journalist and struggling freelance to the most acclaimed young dramatist to emerge since Harold Pinter. I first heard of him in 1965 when I reviewed two of his early radio plays for a Radio 3 arts magazine. (I recall mentioning this fact at the time to a now-distinguished opera producer whose instant reaction was a disdainful 'I know Tom Stoppard – he's a punk journalist from Bristol.') Two years later, on the strength of *Rosencrantz and Guildenstern Are Dead* at the Old Vic, Stoppard was, if not a household name, at least part of the common critical vocabulary. But, amongst Stoppard's early *oeuvres*, there is a far more original work than that which tells us a lot more about his recurrent obsessions and for me summons up much of the spirit of the Sixties: his novel, *Lord Malquist and Mr Moon*. But perhaps it is best to trace the development of the young Stoppard stage-by-stage.

A Walk on the Water (Enter a Free Man)

Every writer has to start somewhere; and the commonest

16

practice is to start with a flagrantly autobiographical play or novel rooting around in the author's own private experience. Stoppard, revealingly, starts with a curiously impersonal piece about a failed, self-deceiving, fiftyish inventor, George Riley. Stoppard himself is now fairly dismissive about *Enter a Free Man* (it is easier to refer to it by its later, published title) often calling it 'Flowering Death of a Salesman' since it has elements both of Robert Bolt and Arthur Miller swimming around in it. Stoppard as a young critic in Bristol obviously saw a lot of plays. He also – as he admitted at the Memorial Service for Kenneth Tynan – was fired by Tynan's enthusiasm for *Look Back in Anger* and by the idea of receiving similar plaudits from the great critic: 'He was still on *The Observer* when I started writing and I can say almost without licence that I wrote my first play in order that he might review it: at least opening *The Observer* was an important part of the fantasy which fuelled the operation.'

Nothing wrong with that; but the disappointing thing about Stoppard's first play is that it lacks the fingerprints of originality and traces of zest that would, you feel, have earned him that Sabbath rave. Its hero is a sad, soiled fantasist, a saloon-bar Mitty, who invents things no-one wants: an envelope with gum on both sides of the flap so you can use it twice ('How do you get it back after you've posted it the first time?' his wife perceptively asks), a pipe that will stay lit provided it is smoked upside down, a bottle-opener for which no bottle-top exists. Even when a Heath-Robinson device of a conduit for funnelling rain indoors to water plants shows sings of working, George then discovers there is no means of staunching the rainwater's flow. Economically dependent on the ten-bob weekly pocket-money he receives from his daughter and emotionally dependent on his loyal Persephone, George lives off dreams: dreams of leaving home, of going into partnership with a flash Harry whom he meets in the pub, of absconding to South America with a tarty stripper who turns out to be Harry's girl-friend. All come to nothing; and there is a final suggestion that George's inablity to handle reality has been handed on to his daughter, Linda, who returns from an abortive elopement on discovering her prospective partner was married. In one of the play's better lines, her mother asks 'How-how far did you let him go?' To which the answer is 'Northampton.'

The real weakness is that Stoppard has nothing much to say

about his chosen subject. He does not glorify the life of Riley or say that we are sustained by our illusions; but nor does he put the case for confronting reality. For a young writer, Stoppard is unusually proficient although curiously absent, and the drumming, insistent echoes only remind you how well other writers have handled similar themes. There is a trace of the Ealing Comedy, *The Man in the White Suit*, in George's realisation that stationery firms would not exactly welcome a re-usable envelope: still the idea is not followed through with the cool logic of the movie. Obviously there are familial links between Miller's Willy Loman and Stoppard's George Riley but the whole point of Miller's play is that Willy's dreams are fuelled by a success-oriented society and his consequent failure gives him no place in that society: no such social criticism, or human pain, disturbs the bland surface of the Stoppard play. Again, one is reminded of Ibsen's Hjalmar Ekdal in *The Wild Duck* rattily determining to leave home once he has discovered the lie on which his happiness is built yet at the same time settling down to a comfortable supper: Ibsen's tragi-comic vitality is missing from *Enter a Free Man*. The most interesting echo of all is of a little-known unarguably great novel written by Balzac in 1834: *La Recherche de l'Absolu*. It is about one Balthazar Claes who is prepared to sacrifice the fortune, health and even life of his family in a single-minded pursuit of a magic formula that will turn base metal into gold. It is a miraculous, detailed study of the madness of ungovernable obsession: of the way the pursuit of an elixir turns almost into a sexual craving and of the way in which vows to reform are constantly overturned by the inventive itch. It is a little unfair to compare a novel of genius to a fledgling play. But Balzac's story has passion and power in its study of the psychology of self-destruction: what one hungers for in Stoppard is some hint of engaged concern.

What one does have, more positively, is – in the final stage version – an ability to move fluently between the Riley living-room and the pub; and a few passages of dialogue that have a nonsensical comic vitality vaguely reminiscent of the war-time radio show, ITMA. When Riley and his pub-friend Harry get going, you feel Stoppard beginning to enjoy himself:

HARRY: Country's going to the dogs. What happened to our greatness?

RILEY: Look at the Japanese.
HARRY: Look at the Japanese.
RILEY: The Japanese looks after the small inventor.
HARRY: All Japanese inventors are small.
CARMEN: They's a small people.
HARRY: Very small. Short.
RILEY: The little man.
HARRY: The little people.
RILEY: Look at the transistor.
HARRY: Very small.
RILEY: Japanese.
CARMEN: Gurkhas are short.
HARRY: But exceedingly brave for their size.
CARMEN: Fearless.
RILEY (*furiously*): What are you talking about?

It's not exactly vintage comic dialogue but it has a nice topsy-turvy quality in which an idea is pursued and extended sentence by sentence: the decline of Britain leads eventually to fearless Gurkhas while rationality and sense eventually disappear up a blind alley.

What is most significant – in the light of Stoppard's subsequent development – is his disdain for the diurnal domestic round and his belief that there is some value in a gesture of eccentric defiance, however puny. Stoppard doesn't do anything as firm as take an attitude, but there is an implicit belief in the George Rileys of this world, in the value of individual initiative and in the awfulness of family routine. George's wife, Persephone, is a loyal characterless drudge, his daughter Linda is a sharp-tongued scold and George himself, when asked if he doesn't like his home, gives a pretty bleak answer:

It's not a question of liking or disliking, it's what it does to you . . . it's *nothing*, absolutely nothing. I give nothing, I gain nothing, it is nothing . . . My wife and I and Linda, we get up in the morning and the water is cold . . . fried bread and sausage and tea . . . the steam in the kitchen and the smell of it all and the springs are broken in my chair . . . Linda goes to sell things . . . in Woolworth's . . . cosmetics and toilet things, and we wash up when the kettle boils again . . . and I go to my room . . . and sit there . . . with my pencils and my workbench . . .

19

The language itself is inert and lifeless yet conveys a withering distaste for the lives of quiet banality most people supposedly live; and consequently seems some kind of endorsement for Riley in his futile attempts to escape. On the strength of this first play, no-one would deduce that Stoppard was a particularly original or interesting writer; nothing much happens beyond the crushing of Geroge's fragile dreams of escape, there is a paucity both of scenic invention and of plot. What is striking is an assumption that a man who invents clocks that play 'Rule Britannia' is somehow slightly superior to those who play by the conventional rules. Stoppard's fascination with the exceptional, however, takes some while to flower.

The Dissolution of Dominic Boot

Drama is about a human being reduced to a state of plausible, unstoppable desperation. By that token Stoppard's first radio play, *The Dissolution of Dominic Boot* (a 15-minute piece broadcast in February, 1964) is good drama. It is logical, quirky, inventive and shows an instant grasp of the medium. Far more than *Enter a Free Man*, it has its own distinctive signature. It also has the quality of a nightmare based on some kind of personal experience. Its hero runs up an escalating taxi-fare and dashes round London trying to raise the money to pay it; and it is interesting to note that Stoppard's agent, Kenneth Ewing, once said: 'When I first met him, he had just given up his regular work as a journalist in Bristol and he was broke. But I noticed that even then he always travelled by taxi, never by bus.'

The play is really a compressed, concertina'd farce based on remorseless arithmetic progression. It starts with the impecunious Boot taking a taxi he can ill afford at the behest of a fiancée he clearly doesn't like. He can't find the two-and-threepence fare. So he takes the cab on to a succession of banks where he is overdrawn, to his office, to his mother's, to a friend in East Croydon, to his father in Windsor and back to the librarian-fiancée who started it all and whom he irrevocably insults. To appease the cab-driver he raids his gas-meter, barters his fiancée's returned engagement-ring and sells his desk, his bed, his wardrobe and finally his suit. He ends up with nothing but a pair of pyjamas and a raincoat as he is forced once more by a female colleague into taking a taxi.

Stoppard's play (which might have been devised by a contemporary urban Lewis Carroll) tells us several things. It shows his grasp of the basic fact that much good farce (and tragedy) springs from a combination of character and logic: one initial miscalculation leads inexorably to disaster whether it be *Charley's Aunt* or *King Lear*. It also reveals Stoppard's awareness (maybe harking back to *The Gamblers*) of prisoner and gaoler: the cabbie and his fare have by the end established a position of total inter-dependence with the former calling the latter by his Christian-name. But what the piece most clearly depicts is Stoppard's instinct for radio. Television would drain the play of plausibility through its narrow literalism (though it was expanded and turned into a film in 1970 called *The Engagement*); as a short-story it would seem contrived; but it works perfectly on radio when you hear the sound of the idling taxi-engine as the hero makes his frantic stops and the noise of the meter ticking over relentlessly.

Radio is one of the great unsung dramatic mediums. It unfetters the dramatist's imagination, allows him to use multiple locations, voices and sounds and permits the listener the dignity of painting his own pictures. BBC Radio, specifically, has always acted as a powerful dramatic patron and in the 1950s and 60s produced a formidable body of work from writers like Giles Cooper, Harold Pinter and John Mortimer. Stoppard figures in that impressive list; and what is significant is that the medium's precise and calculated time-slots act as a necessary container for his sometimes over-spilling imagination. I wouldn't make exaggerated claims for *The Dissolution of Dominic Boot*. But the varied locations and short scenes create a sense of building catastrophe and the play shows how a man can be destroyed through a combination of weakness of character and inexorable mathematical progression.

M is for Moon among Other Things

Stoppard's flair for the wireless and his fascination with logic and order surface again in this play which, like its predecessor, went out in a 15-minute slot, *Just Before Midnight*, in early 1964. It also adumbrates one of Stoppard's recurrent themes: the attempt of human beings to find some pattern or scheme that will somehow shape and explain the meaningless flux of existence. Michael Frayn was later to pursue this theme in plays like *Alphabetical Order* (set in a newspaper-library) and *Benefactors* (in part about the attempt to impose tower-blocks on the unruly chaos of London). But where Frayn puts the case for a certain amount of cheerful disorder, Stoppard himself – rather like his characters – seems to be yearning for something to counteract the random-ness of experience. All art is, by definition, an attempt to order chaos, but Stoppard brings a librarian's zeal to the business of coding and arrangement. He is often praised for his freewheeling exuberance: deep down, I suspect, he's a writer who loves order and control.

You see this in this strange play (strange, that is, for a young writer) about a barren, middle-aged marriage. Alfred, the husband, is a discontented dreamer who immerses himself in lubricious court-reports in the paper and who fantasizes about the consolation he might have been able to offer Marilyn Monroe (the play takes place on the date of her death: August 5, 1962). Constance, his wife, is a pattern-seeker who is trying to encompass human knowledge with the help of a part-work encyclopaedia (she's currently got 'M' to 'N') and who has a very precise consciousness of time, even to the extent of knowing that at half-past-ten she'll be 42½ years old.

What Stoppard is writing about here is the way people attempt to compensate for the disappointments of middle-age and for the sensation of life passing them by. Alfred takes refuge in semi-masturbatory fantasy: Constance in the definition of things from Macedonia to Mumps. What is significant is the absence of up-front compassion (Stoppard is never a bleeding-heart writer) and Stoppard's interest in the codifying Constance. Her husband is ordinary, sensual man. Constance is a natural eccentric. She can't cope with reality: she has caused a domestic disturbance by serving meat to the Catholic wife of her husband's boss on a Friday. She hopes she can get a purchase on experience through the classification of human knowledge. As she says:

'It's lovely to know that every month there's another volume coming. That's the seventh, counting the 'A' to 'B' I got on the actual day. It's 'O' to 'P' this month. Oranges and Orang-utans. I don't know – it's just that the time isn't all a waste, somehow, do you know what I mean?'

I think Stoppard rather sympathises with Constance and that he too enjoys patterns and sequences. This whole play, for instance, is constructed around the letter 'M'. 'M' is for the moon that Constance isn't actually seeking. It's for Marilyn Monroe whose death nourishes Alfred's consolatory dreams. It's for Millie which is Constance's favoured middle-name. And it comes as no surprise that the film showing on television that night is *Dial M for Murder* (though I suppose it could have been Fritz Lang's *M*). Young Tom himself, it is clear, is a bit of a pattern-making word-player and not one of your raw-slice-of-life dramatists.

The play is not as inventive or memorable as its immediate predecessor. But it does exploit one of the things that radio can do best: the constrast between people's spoken and unspoken thoughts. On stage, this is always a tricky device. O'Neill used it to lengthy effect in *Strange Interlude*. Alan Ayckbourn in 1969 employed it in a short play called *Countdown* to highlight the sterility of a middle-aged marriage. Stoppard here uses it intelligently to show that Alfred can relate to a dead film-star ('Well, it's nice to have someone you know you can count on any time, isn't it?') but not to his living wife; and that Constance may not have much joy in her existence ('Every time it's half-past ten, it's another day older and all I've done with it is to get up and stay up. Where's it all going?') At least Constance has her encyclopaedic listings to keep her warm. Despite its theme, it's not a play with a warm, pulsating heart, though Stoppard uses radio very adroitly to show the gap between humdrum outward conversation and the consolation of private dreams.

If You're Glad I'll Be Frank

Stoppard's fascination with the structures we impose on unruly life takes a slightly different turn in his next radio play, *If You're Glad I'll Be Frank*, broadcast on the Third Programme in February, 1966 and originally intended as part of a series about non-existent jobs called *Strange Occupations*. Stoppard seizes on the idea of a bus-driver, Frank, trying to contact his wife, Glad, who is the voice of the speaking-clock, and seeking to rescue her from some Post Office eyrie in which he fancies she is held captive. The point of the play is that we are all prisoners of Time: the victim of timetables, schedules, programmes that govern every waking minute of our existence. If the play has a point, it is to remind us that Time is both a philosophical concept and an arbitrary invention parcelling up every day into hours, minutes and seconds; and that we should seek to be its masters rather than its slaves.

Almost every poet and playwright in history has ruminated on Time. Shakespeare was obsessed by it. Sometimes, as in *Troilus and Cressida*, where it is a 'devouring cormorant' he sees it as mercilessly active; at others, as in *All's Well That Ends Well* where he refers to 'The inaudible and noiseless foot of Time' he sees it as a barely-perceived witness to human affairs. T.S. Eliot, whose lapidary verse-form Stoppard consciously echoes in the play famously wrote in *Ash Wednesday*:

> 'Time present and time past
> Are both perhaps present in time future
> And time future contained in time past.
> If all time is eternally present
> All time is unredeemable.'

J.B. Priestley in his famous 'Time' plays went on to question the notion of Time as a sequential chronology and to show how, in human affairs, there is a constant sense of recurrence and repetition.

Stoppard here says he started out from a much simpler premise. 'I simply liked the central image of the TIM girl being a real person.' Not only does he make Glad a real person but someone who has been driven to breakdown by her omniscient, almost Olympian vision of time and its impartial, disinterested progress:

> 'Of course, it's a service if you like.
> They dial for twenty second's worth of time
> and hurry off contained within it
> until the next correction
> with no sense of its enormity, none,
> no sense of their scurrying insignificance:
> only the authority of my voice,
> the voice of the sun itself,
> more accurate than Switzerland –
> definitive,
> divine.

24

Glad is someone who has grasped the idea of infinitude and who therefore sees all human activity *sub specie aeternitatis*; and what is interesting is how she reinforces that constant strain in Stoppard's early work of aloof disregard for the diurnal, the mundane, the everyday. It's there in *Enter A Free Man* with its explicit distrust for the nine-to-five life. And it's there again in Glad's 'scurrying insignificance' which suggests that all human affairs are without weight and value. You may say those are perfectly reasonable words to put in the mouth of a character whose profession is time. But it makes you wonder if Stoppard himself doesn't share that same dislike of the dreary daily round. What is also interesting about Glad is that her mystical insights have led her towards the sisterhood but her inability to believe that Jesus was the son of God has prevented her becoming a nun: a satirical reference, I suspect, to Dr John Robinson whose book, *Honest to God*, caused a stir in the mid-Sixties through its questioning of similar fundamental tenets of belief.

Glad wants serenity, clean linen and human beings to break through their 'alarm-setting, egg-timing, train-catching, coffee-breaking' existence to a true awareness of Time. And the point is reinforced by the way everyone else in the play is at the desperate mercy of the clock. Frank parks his bus outside the Post Office building for precisely-calculated seconds while he tries to rescue Glad like some medieval knight trying to pluck a damzel from a lofty tower. He, too, is governed by a temporal routine ('Frank – it's 9.14 – remember the schedule' cries his impatient conductress). And the First Lord of the Post Office sets his new secretary (the old one cracked at 1.53 a.m.) the task of keeping constant check on the manifold telephone services ('We can't afford to lose track of time or we'd be lost'). Impishly, Stoppard includes amongst the services (and these were the days when London exchanges had letters, not numbers) 'GOD-dial-the-Bible-reading.' British Telecom has today caught up with Stoppardian satire, you can dial Spaceline for 'Space mission information' (a service for astronauts?) and Skiline for 'Skiing conditions at the principal Scottish ski-centres'. Even Timeline is advertised through an hour-glass dialling a number.

But what exactly is it that makes this an exceptionally promising play by a young writer? Partly it is Stoppard's ability to introduce philosophical concepts into the form of a comic half-hour radio play. Through Glad he is putting forward the idea that in our diurnal rush we overlook the sense of our insignificance in the larger perspectives of Time and Space: if you want to pin it down to a message it is really that of Marcus Aurelius in his *Meditations*: 'In the life of a man, his time is but a moment, his being an incessant flux, his senses a dim rushlight, his body a prey to worms, his soul an unquiet eddy, his fortune dark and his fame doubtful.'

Stoppard is – even this early in his career – conducting a play-by-play debate about how we should order our lives. A part of him (glimpsed in *M Is For Moon*) admits the need for some kind of artificial structure to alleviate our disappointments; another part of him (through the mouthpiece of disintegrating Glad) suggests that such structures can also be constricting and meaningless. Stoppard is not, at this stage, a dramatist of burning convictions: rather, a faintly whimsical explorer of alternative attitudes to life.

He has also quickly learned the advantages of radio and has by-passed entirely cup-and-saucer realism. *If You're Glad I'll Be Frank* is a conceit, a playwith (to use Coleridge's term), a device to pursue ideas. And I well recall that on radio much of its effect came from the contrast between the mechanical tones of Patsy Rowlands as the looped, speaking-clock and the human pain of her attempt to break the time-barrier. Twenty years on, I also still recall Timothy West as distraught Frank trying to contact his imprisoned Glad and bursting into Post-Office boardrooms. The play can be staged (it was indeed done at the Young Vic in 1976) but its virtues are those of radio with its almost surreal transitions and its ability to explore the gap between what we say and what we feel.

A Separate Peace

Stoppard's first three radio plays made a tiny dent in critical consciousness and showed him to be a quirky, off-beat, humorous writer. It would be too grand to talk of preoccupations but one could say he was a dramatist interested in people unable to cope with too much reality, people who erect defence-mechanisms against the world, people who despise or stand outside the drudgery of the daily round. Stoppard was writing in the mid-60s at a time of considerable political turbulence and social change: the Americans had begun bombing North

26

Vietnam, racial riots had erupted in the Watts section of Los Angeles, the Vatican Council had called for the modernization of the Catholic Church, *Time* magazine had asked if God was dead and had discovered Swinging London while the Beatles had erupted all over British life. There was no reason why any of this should find its way into Stoppard's work; but even his early plays hint that modern life is too much and that the best thing is to escape – with whatever grace one can muster – from the surrounding chaos.

That is certainly the path taken by the hero of Stoppard's half-hour television play, *A Separate Peace*, transmitted by BBC-2 in August, 1966 (something of a golden summer for Stoppard since it saw his first major stage play discovered on the Edinburgh Fringe and the publication of his first novel). Stoppard himself has recounted how the play was written as part of an hour-long TV programme in which a documentary and a play were supposed to illuminate each other. The documentary was about chess. But, in Stoppard's words, 'the play, which is about a man escaping from the world (into hospital) does not in fact illuminate what I think about chess players, in whom aggression is probably more important than a desire to escape, but I persuaded myself that this, the only idea I had at the time for a play, fitted well enough.'

If the play illuminates anything, it is Stoppard's preoccupation with fugitives from reality. John Brown, the hero, checks into a superior nursing-home in the early hours of the morning. He is not ill: he simply wants peace, privacy, clean linen, the anonymous freedom provided by a perfectly-run institution. In a hotel, they would want to know why you were staying in bed all day: in a hospital, it is expected of you. But Stoppard shows how society cannot permit such flight. The doctor who mistakenly admitted Brown spends hours on the phone trying to trace his origins; a nurse, Maggie, is sent to spy on him and encourage him in therapeutic painting; and when Brown admits he has been to the hospital before, his relatives are traced and he speedily departs saying 'Trouble is, I've always been so *well*. If I'd been *sick* I would have been all right.'

There have been many fine works of art about congenital nay-sayers: people who choose not to play society's game. Herman Melville's short-story *Bartleby the Scrivener* (1856) is about a copier of legal documents who, whenever asked to undertake a

27

job, says 'I would prefer not to.' Ivan Goncharov's masterly *Oblomov* (1859) is about a hero who disdains to get out of bed. Society, suggests Stoppard, is no more tolerant now than it was a century ago of the passive, the inert, of those who prefer not-doing. Even so, Stoppard's play doesn't add up – or even particularly quicken one's interest – for a variety of reasons.

One is that a man with a suitcase full of money who wanted to achieve serene escape wouldn't really have any great problem in checking into a private nursing-home: he would simply have to lay claim to stress, fatigue or some mild, psychic disorder to gain admittance. But, more crucially, Stoppard never really uses the story to make any point about the horrors of the everyday. Goncharov's hero is a Tsarist absentee landlord who has tried getting up in the past and now doesn't see any point in it; and his apathy strikes fear into the hordes of friends and relations who try to persuade him of the virtues of action. Why get up? Why go out? Why go abroad? Why be polite? Why get married? Those are the questions posed by Oblomov's inaction; and the point of the story is that, when you come down to it, it is very hard to think of a convincing answer.

Stoppard's dessicated piece provokes no such criticism. His hero is a man with no past, no memory, no dreams, no desires except that of retreat. All we really learn is that he was once a POW and has a nostalgia for order:

'Funny thing, that camp. Up to then it was all terrible. Chaos – all the pins must have fallen off the map, dive bombers and bullets. Oh dear, yes. The camp was like breathing out for the first time in months. I couldn't believe it. It was like winning, being captured. The war was still going on but I wasn't going to it any more. They gave us food, life was regulated, in a box of earth and wire and sky.'

The hero is basically an existential cipher and we never learn just what he is escaping from; Stoppard focuses on the institutional panic his decision causes and never goes beyond that to any criticism of life itself. He suggests we don't readily put up with escape, but never presses the point home to explore why we are so scared of people who deny the routine of work, family relationships or the basic connections of society. He sets up a situation and then extends it without investigating it.

28

I don't wish to berate a play written to fill out a commission. This piece has neither the comedy of Goncharov nor the tragedy of Beckett's novels whose heroes, such as Murphy, undergo voluntary seclusion. What it does have is an *unquestioned* assumption that the world is too much with us and that any kind of withdrawal is somehow brave. It may well be: but I want a writer to tell me why, and all Stoppard really offers us in this caprice on solitude is some suave Wildean phrase-making from his hero:

> 'The point is not breakfast in bed but breakfast in bed without guilt – if you're not ill. Lunch in bed is more difficult, even for the rich. It's not any more expensive, but the disapproval is harder to ignore. To stay in bed for tea is almost impossible in decent society, and not to get up at all would probably bring in the authorities. But in a hospital it's not only understood – it's expected. That's the beauty of it.'

A Separate Peace is a harmless fantasy about escape: the kind of daydream we all have at some time of shedding our past and all our emotional luggage. By failing to engage with the kind of society his hero is fleeing from, Stoppard is in the position of a man locking the door on a gaping void. You can have a good play about a man escaping the world; but not, I suggest, one about a man fleeing from nothingness.

Rosencrantz and Guildenstern Are Dead

Stoppard's next produced play, *Rosencrantz and Guildenstern Are Dead*, catapulted him into celebrity and was greeted with the kind of hosannas that a young writer dreams of. Irving Wardle in *The Times* called it 'an amazing piece of work' and 'a gravity-defying masterpiece'. Harold Hobson in *The Sunday Times* dubbed it 'the most important event in the British professional theatre of the last nine years'. Tom was the Boy Wonder who one minute was a struggling unknown, the next a brilliant debutant having his work produced by Olivier's National Theatre Company at the Old Vic. It was a perfect fable for the fame-hungry Sixties. The truth, of course, was a good deal more complex than that. *Rosencrantz and Guildenstern Are Dead* was the product of a longish gestation period; and I believe that it has been as much over-praised as the author's earlier radio work has been under-praised. It is a clever and ingenious play and a startling work to come from a young writer without being the fully-fledged masterpiece many have claimed.

The idea of a play about Shakespeare's attendant lords in *Hamlet* was implanted by Stoppard's agent, Kenneth Ewing, who had the faintly whimsical notion that on arriving in England bearing a sealed message they would find themselves in a country ruled by King Lear. In the spring of 1964 Stoppard was one of four British playwrights given a Ford Foundation grant to spend six months in West Berlin apparently to show the generosity of American support for European art. On the shore of the Wannsee Stoppard wrote a one-act verse comedy, *Rosencrantz and Guildenstern Meet King Lear* which was given a one-night production by English amateur actors in Berlin. It was also given a brief outing by the Questors Theatre in Ealing. Suitably encouraged, Stoppard expanded the piece, turned it from verse into prose and submitted it to the RSC. They took an option on the first two completed acts with the idea of playing it in tandem with David Warner's *Hamlet*. Unsatisfied with the final act, they let the option lapse. Stoppard then tried Frank Hauser at the Oxford Playhouse, who decided he couldn't do it but passed it on to the Oxford Theatre Group, a student company who each year presented a new play on the Fringe of the Edinburgh Festival. In August 1966 the play was premiered at the Cranston Street Hall in Edinburgh. Ronald Bryden in *The Observer* gave it an unqualified rave ('The most brilliant debut by a young playwright since John Arden's'), which prompted Kenneth Tynan, then Literary Manager of the National Theatre, to send off a telegram requesting a script. Within a week the National Theatre had bought it; and, partly because a scheduled, all-male version of *As You Like It* had run into problems, Stoppard's play was quickly put into production and made its debut at the Old Vic on 11 April, 1967. The press, despite doubts expressed by *The Guardian* and *The Daily Telegraph*, was enthusiastic and, rather like Byron, Tom Stoppard woke up one morning and found himself famous.

He was not, as the National's programme generously acknowledged, the first writer to be fascinated by Shakespeare's enigmatic lords. Oscar Wilde in *De Profundis* claimed they were as immortal as Angelo and Tartuffe: 'They are what modern life has contributed to the antique ideal of friendship . . . They are types fixed for all time.' W.S. Gilbert in 1891 wrote a brief burlesque, *Rosencrantz and Guildenstern* in which the former emerges as Hamlet's rival for Ophelia who offers some choice theories about the Prince's mental state ('Hamlet is idiotically sane with lucid intervals of lunacy'). And T.S. Eliot (like Wilde a constant influence on Stoppard) in 'The Love Song of J. Alfred Prufrock' dwelt on the plight of the attendant lord: 'One that will do/To swell a progress, start a scene or two,/Advise the prince; no doubt an easy tool,/Deferential, glad to be of use,/Politic, cautious and meticulous.'

It is fair to say, however, that Stoppard is the first dramatist to build a whole play out of two peripheral theatrical figures. What he shows us is two men with no memory of the past, no understanding of the present and no idea where they are going caught up in a series of incomprehensible events at Elsinore, but Stoppard quickly demolishes the idea that they are interchangeable nonentities. In Act One Stoppard shows them tossing coins which invariably come down Heads: for the incurious, stolid, Watson-like Rosencrantz this is no more than an interesting coincidence while for the ratiocinative, Holmesian Guildenstern it is the source of considerable fear. 'Fear,' he furiously cries. 'The crack that might flood your brain with light.' Stoppard keeps up this distinction for the rest of the act and indeed the whole play. When Rosencrantz and Guildenstern encounter the Players, it is Guildenstern who seeks for some meaningful portent and finds only 'a comic pornographer and a rabble of prostitutes.' Again, when Claudius and Gertrude sweep imperiously on, it is Guildenstern who tries to puzzle some meaning out of the encounter and who sees the universal implications of their dilemma: 'What a fine persecution – to be kept intrigued without ever being enlightened . . .'

Stoppard's Rosencrantz has his own acuity. Immediately after their encounter with Hamlet at the start of Act Two, he sees that their attempt to elicit information by question-and-answer has been an abject failure, but it is always Guildenstern who looks for the universal implications in their dilemma, who sees the need for a belief in some kind of order and appreciates the pathos of their adrift existence:

'We cross our bridges when we come to them and burn them behind us, with nothing to show for our progress except a memory of the smell of smoke, and a presumption that once our eyes watered.'

Guildenstern also pinpoints the essential difference between themselves and the Players, whose leader is the only person at Elsinore who will speak to them. The Players, by their profession, have fixed functions and identities; Rosencrantz and Guildenstern, in contrast, have no past, present and future and exist only through other people's definition of them:

> PLAYER: You can't go through life questioning your situation at every turn.
>
> GUILDENSTERN: But we don't know what's going on, or what to do with ourselves. We don't know how to *act*.

Admittedly it is Rosencrantz who introduces perhaps the most chilling, single thought in the whole play – 'Whatever became of the moment when one first knew about death?' – but it is Guildenstern who elaborates on the subject of death and who sees that dramatic recreations of death bear no relation to the real thing which is simply an ignominious failure to reappear: that one is here one minute and gone the next. The whole second half of the play, in fact, becomes an inexorable progress towards extinction: from, indeed, the ingenious moment when Stoppard extends *The Murder of Gonzago* forward in time so that it foreshadows the moment when Hamlet puts into the hands of the two spies a letter that seals their own deaths.

In the third act – set on the boat bound for England – Stoppard cleverly weaves in the plot of Shakespeare's play, and, we see Hamlet switching the letters that doom the attendant lords to death. Throughout this act, through all the word-games, all the doubts about the reality of England and what they will do when they arrive there, he preserves the vital distinction between the bewildered, supportive Rosencrantz and the speculative, questioning, Socrates-quoting Guildenstern. Both are caught in the familiar human trap of seeming to possess free will while being at the mercy of erratic, unpredictable events that they do not understand. Even when their end is staring them in the face they behave characteristically. It is Rosencrantz who suggests one might as well 'be happy' while it is Guildenstern who, in melancholy cadences, articulates the inevitable: 'We've travelled too far and our momentum has taken over: we move idly towards eternity, without possibility of reprieve or hope of explanation.' Stoppard gives his two heroes distinct personalities but the same fate; and his play follows the progress of two men, summoned at dawn by a mysterious messenger, hustled into a court whose politics they barely comprehend, instructed to tease out the secret of a Prince whose behaviour has puzzled everyone and, finally, despatched towards a dusty, incomprehensible death.

Stoppard's play works on two distinct levels: as an extended gloss upon *Hamlet* which reveals the private dilemma of two attendant lords, and as a metaphor of the human condition showing how we are sent into this world with free will but find ourselves the victim of arbitrary circumstances which lead to our inevitable extinction. On neither level does it seem entirely satisfactory.

Take the play firstly as an example of Shakespeare-as-folklore: an ingenious variation on an original work. It obviously depends on a close acquaintanceship with the original play: I can't imagine it having much resonance in a culture where *Hamlet* was not played year in, year out. More seriously, Stoppard's Rosencrantz and Guildenstern are not a development of Shakespeare's characters but entirely different entities. There's a famous joke in Shakespeare's play where Claudius and Gertrude echo their compliments to the two lords (which many directors take as a sign of their total indistinguishability); but Shakespeare's Rosencrantz and Guildenstern are not mere ciphers, they are two men who have had a past relationship with Hamlet, have been summoned to court to sus out his distemper and who are rather brutally despatched by him. Indeed what is striking is how fulsomely greeted they are on arrival at Elsinore. 'Welcome, dear Rosencrantz and Guildenstern/Moreover that *we much did long to see you,*/The need we have to use you did provoke/Our hasty sending.' (my italics) What do those lines imply if not that they are regular and extremely welcome visitors to the court? 'Something have you heard/Of Hamlet's trans-formation; . . .' continues Claudius which again implies that they are near enough to the court to pick up the gossip. Most crucially, Claudius says 'I entreat you both,/That, being of so young days brought up with him/And sith so neighboured to his youth and haviour,/That you vouchsafe your rest here in our court/Some little time.' These are clearly not men plucked out of darkness to investigate Hamlet's madness: these are old, trusted chums who have already been summoned for a specific purpose.

Stoppard, to his credit, includes that scene in his play. If you listen to the lines carefully, however, they provide little justification for the panic Rosencrantz and Guildenstern feel on Claudius's departure in Stoppard's version. They may be caught up in something of a state crisis; but they are hardly nobodies asked to dissect the madness of a man they have never met before. As many critics have pointed out, Stoppard also carefully omits the post-play scene in Act 3 Scene 2 where Guildenstern is sent to summon Hamlet to Gertrude's closet. He omits it because it would overturn his vision of Rosencrantz and Guildenstern as mystified, puzzled figures at the mercy of events. What is striking about Shakespeare's scene is how purposeful Rosencrantz and Guildenstern are and how it is Hamlet who is distraught and manic. Guildenstern tries the firm, heavy-handed approach: 'Good my lord, put your discourse into some frame and start not so wildly from my affair.' Rosencrantz tries the softly-softly tactic: 'My lord, you once did love me . . . Good my lord, what is your distemper? You do surely bar the door upon your own liberty, if you deny your griefs to your friend.' These are hardly the words of anonymous attendants. And this exchange leads to that famous passage in which Hamlet rounds on the two lords and asks Guildenstern to play on the recorder. Why does he do this? To make the point that Guildenstern would seek to play upon him, to pluck out the heart of his mystery, to sound him from the lowest note to the top of his compass: Guildenstern cannot play the recorder but he seeks to delve Hamlet's mystery. 'Sblood, do you think I am easier to be play'd on than a pipe?' Hamlet thus turns the tables on a couple of manipulative ex-friends. To have included that scene would have overturned Stoppard's whole thesis that Rosencrantz and Guildenstern are mystified figures uncertain of their own identities.

There is no obligation on Stoppard to simply extend Shakespeare's characters realistically beyond the life of the play. He is artistically free to make of them what he pleases, but it is Stoppard himself who brings Shakespeare's Hamlet,

Claudius and Polonius onto the stage. Once he does so, one is bound to enquire how they marry up with his invented Rosencrantz and Guildenstern; and the answer is hardly at all. He retains episodes from Shakespeare's play in which Rosencrantz and Guildenstern have a defined purpose and role and are even greeted by Claudius as welcome returnees: he then presents us with two unenlightened, if sympathetic, stumblebums. Stoppard's play was timely in that it came at a moment when the anti-romantic, anti-heroic interpretation of *Hamlet* was suddenly popular. Peter Hall's 1965 production at Stratford with David Warner had established the idea of Elsinore as a network of Machiavellian saboteurs with at the centre a confused, myopic, uncertain Prince. Stoppard's play reinforces the division between the world of sweeping public events and individual perplexity, but his coin-tossing, word-game-playing heroes are more Vladimir and Estragon at Elsinore than the Rosencrantz and Guildenstern implied in Shakespeare's text.

Leaving aside the Shakespeare connection, what does Stoppard's play tell us? We go to theatre for a variety of purposes but the bottom line is that we expect some illumination of human experience: something that tells us what it is like to be alive now or explains what it was like to be alive then. By that token, what is the tangible pleasure offered by *Rosencrantz and Guildenstern Are Dead*?

When the play first appeared it was instantly compared by a good critic, Ronald Bryden, to *Love's Labour's Lost*. That sends us straight off in the wrong direction since Shakespeare's early comedy is a sharp criticism of withdrawal into a world of punning, word-spinning, self-delighting cleverness: almost, if you like, an attack on Stoppardism. Philosophically, Stoppard's play belongs to the tradition of Theatre of the Absurd as defined by Ionesco in an essay on Kafka: 'Absurd is that which is devoid of purpose . . . Cut off from his religious, metaphysical and transcendental roots, man is lost: all his actions become senseless, absurd, useless.'

That is an almost copybook description of the plight of Stoppard's two heroes. They are confronted by an inexplicable world in which a coin may come down Heads ninety-two times. They are left waiting in an antechamber to fill in time while people rush in and out plying them with instructions they don't fully understand. They are unsure of their own names, of any past experience, of what exactly they are meant to do, of how precisely to pass the time. All they do really know is that they were peremptorily sent for:

> Guildenstern: A man standing in the saddle in the half-lit half-alive dawn banged on the shutters and called two names. He was just a hat and a cloak levitating in the grey plume of his own breath but when he called we came. That much is certain – we came.

Somewhere, somehow, Guildenstern assumes, there may be some logic and order that explains their situation. They have no access to it; and, in the meantime, they are at the mercy of whatever happens and whoever comes on next:

ROSENCRANTZ: What are you playing at?
GUILDENSTERN: Words, words. They're all we've got to go on.

Pause.

ROSENCRANTZ: Shouldn't we be doing something constructive?
GUILDENSTERN: What did you have in mind? . . . A short, blunt human pyramid . . .?
ROSENCRANTZ: We could go.
GUILDENSTERN: Where?
ROSENCRANTZ: After him.
GUILDENSTERN: Why? They've got us placed now – if we start moving around, we'll all be chasing each other all night.

Hiatus

ROSENCRANTZ (*at footlights*): How very intriguing. (*Turns.*) I feel like a spectator – an appalling prospect. The only thing that makes it bearable is the irrational belief that somebody interesting will come on in a minute . . .
GUILDENSTERN: See anyone?
ROSENCRANTZ: No. You?
GUILDENSTERN: No. (*At footlights.*) What a fine

persecution – to be kept intrigued without ever being quite enlightened.

Stoppard's play seems to be making a very basic, philosophical point: that for most of us life, like laughter, is something going on in the next room, that if there is a system and order to human affairs it is never readily apparent and that the only certainties are birth and death. As Guildenstern says: 'The only beginning is birth and the only end is death – if you can't count on that, what can you count on?' Which of course evokes memories of one of the most famous lines in *Waiting For Godot*: 'We are born astride a grave.'

My problem with all this is that Beckett in *Waiting For Godot* explored to the limit the notion of a meaningless universe in which we pass the time as best we may. Beckett showed how we doze, bicker, invent games, take little conversational canters – do anything to stave off the void and the ultimate mystery of existence. I can't help feeling that all Stoppard has done is take the commonplaces of the Absurd and transfer them to a new setting which is the outer fringe of an existing play. On top of this, the play seems like a virtuoso conjuring-trick in which Stoppard builds a three-hour drama out of next-to-nothing but in which you feel his presence for ever skilfully manipulating the characters. That, in essence, is the problem. On the one hand, Rosencrantz and Guildenstern are bewildered innocents; on the other, they are (especially Guildenstern) bright, sharp, mercurial, philosophical and ever so self-aware. They are Stoppard's creatures and there are only a few moments when he lets go of them and gives them some kind of independent existence. They fill the void with talk: but it is Stoppard-talk of an erudite, knowing kind. Yes, they are characters without a past; but they are clever enough to refer to Chinese philosophers of the T'ang Dynasty and to Socrates. They don't know who they are or why they are, but it is they themselves who constantly define their problem with a remorseless self-consciousness.

It is a clever play. But it cannot sustain its length. When I saw Derek Goldby's production at the Old Vic in 1967, I remember being hooked by the surface brilliance but, at the same time, being aware of the way the impetus and momentum ebbed simply because the characters were incapable of extension and because of a felt aridity at the idea that the universe was senseless. I was more engaged by Bernard Goss's much simpler, cleaner production at the Young Vic in 1974. But, studying the play again now, I feel that the wordplay is overstretched, that a one-act idea is being teased out and that the essential innocence of truly great drama is missing. Beckett's *Waiting For Godot* has a continuing resonance because his characters are simpler, more naïve, less resourceful, more poetic and, of course, go on bravely waiting. Stoppard's play is, I suspect, less durable because it has less real human content and because its puzzled heroes take on something of the alertness of their author who is pulling the all-too-visible strings.

Lord Malquist and Mr Moon

It is worth asking what deductions one would make about Stoppard as a writer at this stage of his career. They would be:

That he had a fascination with detached, alienated, outsiderish heroes and heroines (George Riley, Glad, John Brown, Rosencrantz and Guildenstern) who either found life mysterious or impossible to cope with.

That Stoppard heroes often erect, as a protection against the teeming mayhem of life, some precarious order of their own to make temporary sense of things.

That each of the plays revolves around a bizarre central conceit: an escalating, unpayable taxi-fare, a suffering soul trapped inside the speaking-clock, a woman remorselessly working her way through an encyclopaedia of human knowledge, a healthy man who retreats into a hospital, an oblique sidelong vision of life at Elsinore from two attendant lords.

That Stoppard's literary heroes are an odd mixture of T.S. Eliot, Oscar Wilde, Samuel Beckett and Lewis Carroll, with whom he shares a fascination with arithmetical logic.

That Stoppard owes little to the ingrained realism of British drama, that he views human affairs with slightly Olympian detachment, that he sees plays (unlike many of his contemporaries) not as vehicles for personal statements but as highly-conscious artefacts.

That he is a highly ingenious, cerebral writer with a flair for verbal wit that sometimes shades into whimsicality.

That he is a brilliantly resourceful writer for radio but that his one major stage play leaves you (or, more accurately, leaves me) hungering for rather more in the way of flesh-and-blood humanity.

The irony to me is that Stoppard's ascent to fame depended on the Oxford Theatre Group production of *Rosencrantz and Guildenstern Are Dead* in August 1966 whereas the same month saw the publication of his first (and only) novel *Lord Malquist and Mr Moon* which sank without trace. The play is clever but derivative: the novel strikes me as one of the most original published in England since the war. Stoppard himself was clearly somewhat surprised at the hyperbolic reaction to the play and the wilful disregard of the novel. In a *Guardian* interview with Janet Watts (the original Ophelia in *Rosencrantz and Guildenstern*) in 1973 he observed of the Oxford student production: 'I was very light-hearted about the whole thing because I had a novel published in the same week that the play opened and there was no doubt in my mind whatsoever that the novel would make my reputation and that the play would be of little consequence either way.' The play went on to the National Theatre; the novel in its first eight months sold 481 copies and achieved popularity only in Venezuela where they clearly have an appetite for bold fantasy. What this proves is the extraordinary power of the theatre in British culture in the mid-1960s. The Royal Court revolution was ten years old; the National Theatre and the Royal Shakespeare Company were an established fact of life; and the fame-machine demanded a constant supply of new talent to prove that the Osborne-Pinter-Arden-Wesker generation was not a flash in the pan. Stoppard came along at the right moment and one does not begrudge him his acclaim. It just seems unfair – and disproportionate – that Stoppard's work for radio never merited more than the odd paragraph and that his first novel was part of the general processing that goes on in our weekly Books Pages under the guise of reviewing.

What is surprising about *Lord Malquist and Mr Moon* is how little it owes to its precursors in the English novel. Kingsley Amis, John Wain, John Braine had spearheaded a new movement in English fiction that – in parallel with what was happening in the theatre – gave voice to the articulate, dispossessed young, mocked official, cultural attitudes and viewed with a good deal of cynicism the carefully-graded hierarchies of British academic, industrial and artistic life. Even more philosophical writers like Iris Murdoch – who dealt with ethical issues and the vagaries of human passion – still anchored their work in a believable reality. Stoppard's first fiction is the work of a sport with a mind: it is a fizzing, exuberant caprice but one that deals with a plethora of ideas. It also establishes working-methods and particular obsessions that were to fertilise Stoppard's plays over the next decade.

Stoppard's first chapter, 'Dramatis Personae and Other Coincidences', doesn't simply establish the characters. It presents us with a series of apparently unconnected, surrealist events all of which, it transpires, have a rational explanation: a technique Stoppard was to develop later. It bombards us with bizarre sensations – in the manner of a Jackson Pollock painting or, more mundanely, an episode of *The Avengers* – and then allows us to deduce the pattern.

So it begins with a coach careering through London, from Whitehall to Mayfair, at a time of national mourning: its occupants are a stylish, aphoristic aristocrat, Lord Malquist, and a Boswellian scribe, Mr Moon, scarcely noticing that a woman bearing a petition has been mown down in their path. Cut to a left-handed gun on a chestnut mare and a cowboy rival talking in the trimmed, laconic style of John Wayne while apparently riding through a London park. Cut to a drunken, desperate woman tottering wildly about while watched from behind a scrub of thorn by a lion. Cut to a man with thick matted curls and a straggling beard weaving his way through the London crowds on the back of a recalcitrant donkey. Cut to a sexy, pensive, beautiful girl called Jane at her toilette (more truthfully, squatting on the loo) whose meditations are interrupted by the arrival of an importunate, pistol-packing admirer. Cut back to Moon whom, we discover, is carrying a bomb with a time-fuse, who engages in dialogues with himself and who is obsessed with the notion of saving a world that has got out of control. In his own words:

It's all got huge, disproportionate in the human scale, it's all gone rotten because life – I feel it about to burst at the seams because the sheer volume and numbers of the things we're filling it up with and people, it's all multiplying madly and no-one is controlling it because it's all got too *big*.'

40

Who are all these people and what is the connection between them? In succeeding chapters, Stoppard draws the threads together and shows that everything has a rational, if not always, plausible explanation. Lord Malquist himself is an impecunious phrase-maker who sees around him – like many a Stoppard hero – disorder, turmoil and absurdity and who shrugs a world-weary eyebrow. In a much-quoted phrase, he says: 'Since we cannot hope for order let us withdraw with style from the chaos.' Stoppard himself seems haunted by the busy messiness of human activity and he has more than a shred of sympathy with the epigram-toting aristo. Time and again one is reminded of Lord Henry Wootton in Wilde's *The Picture of Dorian Gray* who likewise sees human life through the prism of seductive phraseology. Lord Henry is ever ready with a poisoned jest on the lines of 'Conscience and cowardice are really the same things, Basil. Conscience is the trade-name of the firm. That is all.' Or 'The only difference between a caprice and a life-long passion is that the caprice lasts a little longer.' Stoppard's ninth earl is like a more vigorously heterosexual version of the same character. He devotes his idle days to a project of exquisite triviality, the preparation of a little monograph on *Hamlet* as a source of book-titles. Style for him is everything. He says,

'I would rather my book were unread than ungraceful, don't you know? Do you find writing easy?'
'Well, not yet,' said Moon. 'I haven't got my material together yet.'
'I find it an awful chore. My problem is that I am not frightfully interested in anything except myself. And of all forms of fiction autobiography is the most gratuitous. I am far happier putting my *Life* in your hands.'

Lord Malquist withdraws with style from the chaos: Moon has the desperate ambition to find a meaningful pattern in the random sequence of events we call history. His prime task is writing a monumental history of the world (J.M. Roberts, of course, has actually done it) but although he makes furious notes he cannot quite bring himself to start the first sentence. In the meantime, he has set up a firm called Boswell Inc. and hires himself out for ten guineas a day as a personalised chronicler.

Where Malquist sails through life with sublime disregard, Moon is an agitated, virginal klutz who nurses his home-made bomb in the vain hope that throwing it will somehow draw attention to the impossible human and technical complexity of modern life. Stoppard said in a 1972 *New York Times* interview with Mel Gussow, 'I write plays because writing dialogue is the only respectable way of contradicting yourself.' I sense that is what he is doing here in his creation of Malquist and Moon. One withdraws from the chaos; the other seeks to explain it or to chuck a bomb at it. Stoppard is present himself in both characters which helps to give the novel its dialectical vigour.

But Stoppard does not here theorise about the lunatic chaos of modern life; he actually represents it and, in particular, conveys the charade-like quality of London life in the mid-Sixties when dressing-up and display co-existed with a rather frantic, bogus spirituality. Bernard Levin in *The Pendulum Years* wrote perceptively about the new young aristocracy of the 1960s:

> 'They ate strange food, calling it macro-biotic and seemed to thrive on it; they dabbled in strange religion calling it Zen Buddhism and seemed to grow calm on it; they wore strange clothes, calling them fashionable, and lo the clothes became fashionable among many who had noticed that their exemplars were famous, and perhaps thought that if they imitated them exactly enough they would discover the secret, and that they too would thus become famous, and perhaps not only famous but rich.'

Behind the Biblical cadences Levin hits a truth; and Stoppard's novel is a fascinating testament to a decade in which only the bizarre became predictable. Who exactly are these cowboys, L.J. Slaughter and Jasper Jones, riding through the streets and parks of London like Butch Cassidy and the Sundance Kid? They are not only rivals for the hand (and body) of Moon's wife but part of a campaign for the promotion of pork beans. Who exactly is the man on a donkey? He proclaims himself the Risen Christ and wishes to preach the word to the multitude in St Paul's Cathedral. Who exactly is the drunken shoeless woman tottering about Green Park? She is Lord Malquist's wife, Laura, who has been forcibly ejected from the Ritz and who is watched from behind parkland scrub by Rollo, Lord Malquist's lion who escaped one day while his owner was out riding in Rotten Row. And who, exactly, is the seductive Jane described by Stoppard in such lushly romantic terms ('A painter would have delighted in the peeping blush of her firm young breasts where the thin silk of her gown fell loose about her')? She is Moon's delectable, apparently intact wife who is constantly caught in compromising positions by her insanely jealous husband. All these characters interweave and interact on the eve and during the day of a particularly momentous event: the state funeral of Sir Winston Churchill.

But what is Stoppard actually doing in this novel and just why is it such a heady and potent brew?

He is writing, quite seriously, about contrasting attitudes to the flux of events: stylish disengagement and pattern-seeking. He is pinning down, with a good deal of prophetic accuracy, a particular moment in British life when the man of action was replaced by the spectator and when the last leader apparently to determine the course of events was replaced by people who seemed to be at the mercy of them. He is raising a series of questions about history and placing the deterministic view alongside the individualistic. He is also asking whether all mortal affairs are dictated by random events or an inevitable chain of cause-and-effect. Not least, he is enjoying himself writing a series of parodies that range from Wilde to Wodehouse. He is handling momentous issues with a light-hearted zest and, for the first time, giving meaning to the epithet 'Stoppardian'. What makes it such a good novel is that it breaks free both from prole-realism and the minute depiction of bourgeois crises that dominate English fiction, and shows that something filled with fantasy and wild invention can take on board the serious. It is a *jeu d'esprit* – with a point.

If the phrase 'Stoppardian' came to imply a larkish treatment of ideas, it also came to suggest a wariness of commitment and a distrust of fixed ideologies; a belief shared with Nietzsche that 'convictions are prisons'. But what people discovered in the plays is all there in this novel: it is the blueprint for both *Jumpers* and *Travesties*. Moon, for instance, at one point escapes from the nightmare of his Mayfair mews house – where he discovers Lord Malquist apparently committing cunnilingus with his wife – for a chat with his lordship's coachman: a, literally, black

Irishman by the name of O'Hara. While O'Hara smokes his pipe, Moon unburdens himself of his philosophy:

'I distrust attitudes' he went on, 'because they claim to have appropriated the whole truth and pose as absolutes. And I distrust the opposite attitude for the same reason. O'Hara . . .? You see when someone disagrees with you on a moral point you assume that he is one step behind in his thinking and he assumes that he has gone one step ahead. But I take both parts, O'Hara, leapfrogging myself along the great moral issues, refuting myself and rebutting the refutation towards a truth that must be a compound of two opposite half-truths. And you never reach it because there is always something more to say. But I can't ditch it, you see O'Hara. I can't just align myself with whatever view has the approved moral tone to it. I'm not against black people really, I only recoil from the simplicity of taking up a virtuous position in support of them regardless of the issue. There is nothing so simple as virtue and I distrust simplicity. Anyway, he added lamely, 'I firmly believe in the equality and proportionate decency of all mankind regardless of race or colour. But I wouldn't want my sister to marry a black man. Or a Chinaman or an Algerian. Or an Australian or a Rhodesian or a Spaniard. Or a Mexican or a prison warder or a Communist, though quite often I think there is much to be said for Communism . . . And to tell you the truth, I haven't got anything against anybody. Except perhaps Irishmen. I hate Irishmen.'

'I'm from Dublin myself,' said O'Hara and broke into an old man's cackle.

This is *echt*, early Stoppard and as close as the author probably comes in the book to a statement of his own beliefs. Its virtue is its honesty: its limitation is its flabbiness when applied to particular historical circumstances. Moon distrusts absolutes. He suggests the truth lies in a compound of two opposite half-truths. Stoppard only follows this argument through in so far as it applies to questions of 'Would you let your sister marry a black man?' Apply the Moon line of thinking to some of the momentous events of modern history and its flaw becomes quickly apparent. Where would Moon stand on, for instance, Hitler's determined and calculated campaign to exterminate some six-million Jewish people? Or on Stalin's elimination of some 10 million Russian peasants in order to break resistance to his plans for the collectivization of agriculture? Or on the Afrikaaner Nationalist Party's imposition of *Apartheid* in 1948 with its total separation of races socially, economically and territorially? Moon's rejection of inflexible absolutes sounds moderate and reasonable. But it seems to me a glaring weakness of his – and ultimately Stoppard's position – that there are issues of good and evil in world affairs and many clear-cut occasions when we recoil from abomination. Even if one confines the matter to issues of personal morality, it still seems to me that Moon's argument is weak. 'There is nothing so simple as virtue and I distrust simplicity.' But is it simple to condemn and punish murder, torture, the abuse of children, the persecution of animals, rape, arson, theft and myriad other crimes? Stoppard is too kindly a man not to detest all those things; and this precisely is the point. If he were to see someone being kicked to death in the street, he would not adopt a Moon-like seeing-all-sides-of-the-issue moral ambiguity: he would rush to the person's defence or summon the police. I see what Stoppard is saying through Moon's speech: that it is easy to adopt sanctimonious attitudes to moral questions that bear no relation to human experience; but I believe there is such a thing as an instinctive morality and that it operates all the time in our daily life.

My use of the word 'instinctive' begs a question which Moon himself raises a moment or two later.

'I cannot commit myself to either side of a question,' Moon said. 'Because if you attach yourself to one or the other you disappear into it. And I can't even side with the balance of morality because I don't know whether morality is an instinct or just an imposition.'

This is a question Stoppard goes on to explore in depth in *Jumpers*. For the moment I would simply say that a revulsion against, for instance, the torture of the weak by the strong is not something implanted by the Judaeo-Christian or any other commanding ethic but a common human attribute. But there is an interesting admission by Moon here that to take any kind of stand is somehow to sacrifice one's own uniqueness. It seems to me a nonsensical argument and a testament to human vanity and insecurity rather than anything else. Standing up for a belief, or even participating in a corporate action, is not a desecration of individuality: it may indeed be a summation of it. I no more 'disappear' into a question by taking a particular line than I disappear into a room because it is full of people or disappear into democracy because I choose to exercise my vote. Moon's statement is a poignant exposure of the liberal fallacy though whether Stoppard sees it as such I am not sure.

It says much for the book that it sets off this kind of argument; and the funeral of Sir Winston Churchill (though he is never actually mentioned by name) is central to Stoppard's wish to debate whether history is produced by the chance eruption of events and people or whether there is a discernible pattern. It is difficult, to anyone too young to remember them, to stress how momentous were the days of Churchill's illness, death and funeral in January, 1965. The funeral itself took place on a grey London day but it was unforgettable. Kings, queens, presidents, prime ministers, generals, high commissioners came from all over the world. 25 million people in Britain (half the population) watched the event on television and 350 million people (a tenth of the world's population) saw it throughout the globe. It also, as Bernard Levin emphasises in his book, was a historical watershed for this country: the moment when the idea of national unity and faith in great men, which Churchill had represented, once and for all departed and when Britain shook off its past and confronted an uncomfortable future.

With sublime cheekiness, Stoppard weaves the period of Churchill's final illness, death and funeral into the texture of his novel. Moon first encounters Lord Malquist riding in Hyde Park. At one moment, the falcon Lord Malquist carries on his arm flies off and perches on the roof of a house set back from the road where a fair-sized crowd has gathered. Lord Malquist calls out 'Hillo, Hoho. Hillo, hoho' to attract the bird exciting the crowd's audible disapproval as a figure in white appears at one of the windows. Moon himself is implicated and 'delayed by a hysterical lady who berated me for an act of disrespect towards "the greatest man in the world".'

Even more irreverently, Stoppard uses Churchill's funeral as a backdrop for scenes of macabre farce. In an early chapter of the novel, there are two spectacular deaths: a bullet fired by one of the amorous, insensate cowboys ricochets off the wall of Moon's living-room and kills his wife's French maid, Marie, who is hiding under a *chaise longue*. Moon, half in love with Marie, discovers that she has been running a kinky, photographic model-business from his home and himself kills, by breaking a bottle over his head, a dirty-minded old General who has been taking photographs of Marie's corpse with her dress up over her head. Desperately, Moon bundles the two corpses into a roll of carpet, places them on the back of the Risen Christ's donkey and instructs him to dispose of them; and who, at Churchill's funeral, should come into sight – after the Royal Naval gun-crew, the family mourners, members of the Household Cavalry, the Royal Artillery and the Metropolitan Police – but 'a white-robed figure on a donkey monstrously saddled with a carpet roll.' As if there were not enough, the two cowboys stage a climactic shoot-out, the lion Rollo runs down Whitehall bearing one of the Queen's flamingoes between its teeth and Moon detonates his bomb which releases a swelling red, rubbery, balloon-like bubble that grows to the size of a church-dome and bears across it, in black letters, a two-word message – 'familiar, unequivocal and obscene.' At the climax to 'God Save the Queen' the balloon bursts, pieces of red rubber float over Trafalgar Square and 'a few people, obscurely moved, begin to applaud.'

This is not, however, idle, wanton rudery on Stoppard's part: a defacing of a great moment in history. What Stoppard is doing is underlining Levin's point that the death of Churchill was indeed a watershed in British life: that it marked the passing of an age when, in Lord Malquist's words, history was 'a drama directed by great men' and when the heroic posture was a possibility and ushered in another age that was random, chaotic, violent, even farcical. Stoppard, true to form, does not take sides or say either that he regrets the passing of the old era or the advent of the new, but he forces us to recognise that something of profound significance occurred in Britain in late January, 1965 and that things would never be quite the same thereafter. As W.B. Yeats said after the first night of Alfred Jarry's *Ubu Roi*, 'After us the savage gods.'

Although Stoppard does nothing so vulgar in this amazing book as declare whether he believes history is a series of random happenings or a long chain of cause-and-effect with a Toynbee-esque grand design, his method of writing the book implies that there is something beyond the operation of mere chance in human affairs. He does, in fact, wittily send up the notion of a

47

historical design in a duologue between the earnest Moon and the drunken Laura Malquist. Moon defends his researches into whether all is random or inevitable and then asks:

'But if it's all random then what's the point?'
'What's the point if it's all inevitable?'
'She's got me there.'

On a microcosmic scale, however, Stoppard implies there has to be a purpose and a pattern to human affairs. He himself begins the book with what seems like a series of haphazard occurrences: he also shows a fat lady being ridden down as she attempts to thrust a petition through the window of Lord Malquist's coach. Gradually, the pieces fall into place and we see that Moon's wife is a magnet for the gunslinging cowboys, that the Risen Christ expresses the charming charlatanism of religious fakery, that the disengaged Lord Malquist's lion is gazing upon his master's sottish wife, that Lady Malquist initiates the virginal Moon into the joys of sex and that there is some invisible, subtly-woven thread linking all the characters. But still there is the question of the woman knocked flying at the start of the book. On Page 131 we learn that a Mrs Hermione Cuttle was knocked down and killed in Pall Mall by a runaway coach-and-pair. On Page 185 Lord Malquist writes a letter to *The Times* disclaiming any responsibility for the incident. At the very end of the book, Moon resigns himself to the fact that the pattern in historical affairs has eluded him, that his wife is finally securely closeted with Lord Malquist, that even Lady Malquist has enjoyed the favours of the all-too-literally Risen Christ and that he is a doomed outsider. He rides home in Lord Malquist's caoch and, as it gets to the corner of Birdcage Walk, a Mr Cuttle, assuming the coach contains its rightful owner, tosses a bomb in through the window which blows Moon, the coach and its driver to smithereens.

Which all goes to show that there is a pre-determined pattern in human life. Or, if you prefer, that our fates are dictated by random events.

Teeth

Lord Malquist was planning a small monograph on *Hamlet* as a source of play-titles. I suppose a similar collector of minutiae might offer a tiny pamphlet on the influence of dentistry on drama. It would, of course, include Shaw's *You Never Can Tell* the first act of which is set in the surgery of an impoverished dentist and ends with a patient being given gas before his tooth is extracted. It would continue with Graham Greene's *The Complaisant Lover* which deals with a suburban dentist whose wife is sleeping with a local bookseller and which ends with a proposed *menage à trois*. It would make passing reference to John Mortimer's one-acter, *Muswell Hill*, in which a prosperous Harley Street dentist returns home unexpectedly to find his wife and a fellow-practitioner cavorting round as Queen Elizabeth I and Sir Walter Raleigh. And it would climax in Stoppard's half-hour TV play, *Teeth* (transmitted on February 7, 1967 with John Wood and John Stride) in which a cuckolded dentist extracts not only gruesome revenge on his wife's lover but also his front-tooth in a symbolic form of castration. It may be minor Stoppard; but it pursues his fascination with sexual infidelity, plays on common nightmares about our powerlessness in dentist's chairs and works perfectly at its chosen length.

It also shows Stoppard is a great lover of jokes: inside Stoppard the philosophical Absurdist lurks an Eddie Braben who is not so much screaming to be let out as given full rein. Kingsley Amis once told me that a lot of the motive for writing was 'self-entertainment': with Stoppard that is clearly visible. Thus here he starts in the waiting-room with a chat between two women one of whom, Agnes, lost her lover when he walked into her bathroom without knocking and saw everything: that she was brushing her teeth after dinner. The only problem was they were in her hands at the time. This is a bit like the old George Burns joke about the luscious chorus-girl who has been seen running her fingers through his hair: in fact, he came into his dressing-room and found her doing it. But so appalled was Agnes's lover that 'a week later he'd got his third mate's papers and he was taken away over the horizon by a dirty black tramp – yeh, Irene Castle from Cardiff, I still look out for her.'

Clearly the gag-man cometh. But just occasionally one feels the dialogue is not all that far above the level of a pier-end farce.

When George Pollock, the randy patient whom Stoppard describes as a saloon-bar Lothario, flirts outrageously with the white-coated dental receptionist (who turns out to be his own wife) we get lines like 'You like my smile really – it's one of the two things you like about me.' And when George goes into the surgery for his encounter with the dentist there are nudge-nudge exchanges like:

GEORGE: You won't find much wrong with *my* choppers.
HARRY (*To the wife*): In flashing form is he.

One is reminded that at this juncture in his career there is still a trace of the schoolboy about Stoppard who writes about sex as if it were something thrillingly horrific.

But the play improves radically when George is at Harry's mercy in the dentist's chair. It proceeds, in fact, through a constant series of comic misunderstandings in which Harry is probing George's mouth and uttering dire warnings that could apply equally to his bicuspids or his philanderings with Harry's wife, Prudence:

HARRY: I'm glad you came in today – this is a serious warning, George; you think that people can't see what isn't happening – but it all comes out in the end.

Indeed it does. But, before we reach that point, Stoppard plays ingeniously with the power we surrender to the man with the drill, the sweetness of the cuckold's revenge and the desperate excuses we resort to in order to explain our misdemeanours. The dentist's wife has been seen rowing with George on the Serpentine: what is more she has come home wearing George's wife's shoes. This leads to a series of wriggling explanations by George, a salesman, who claims that he was out demonstrating a rowing-boat to a client, spotted Prudence and offered her a paddle, she got her feet wet and so they nipped back to his place to borrow a pair of his wife's shoes – accompanied by a group of old people whom Prudence ostensibly sees on a Tuesday afternoon. This is the kind of thing of which Ray Cooney is a master – the spiralling, flustered, panic-stricken explanation that gets more and more desperate and improbable as it goes on. Stoppard shows he can handle this kind of sexual farce with compact skill. And he decorates it with his own brand of verbal curlicue – Harry explains that he took revenge on a previous seducer of his wife but that it's all 'water under the bridge now' – and with some neat sight-gags: at one point Harry appears with a mallet and chisel to George's visible terror and then uses it to adjust the head-rest, he applies a green liquid to George's gums and then applies a girder-like clamp to his mouth leaving him with gaping jaws while he and George's wife retreat behind the chair to audibly smooch. The final twist comes when a shaken George emerges gap-toothed into the waiting room only to hear the two women discoursing on the importance of a full set of teeth ('Because if *they've* gone already, what'll go next, I said.') and to confront a set of patients all 'with smiles like broken-down brooms.'

It is a good joke. Stoppard equates sexual magnetism with gleaming molars and shows how the physical disquiet induced by the dentist's chair may be intensified by the vengeful torture of a tromped husband. It is also good television where the close-ups of tools and nozzles for swivelling and drilling add to the sense of impending terror. The play also reminds us of our impotence when we are in the hands of dentists: my own excellent surgeon recently asked me my opinion of *Les Misérables* while my jaws were non-conversationally extended. This is Stoppard the journeyman dramatist showing that he can take a familiar subject – the deceived husband's revenge – and give it a new twist through an ingenious setting and a scattering of visual and verbal jokes. Stoppard is an entertainer as well as an erudite punster: and in this play he provides half an hour of good television.

Another Moon Called Earth

1967 was something of a vintage year for Stoppard. *Rosencrantz and Guildenstern Are Dead* became an instant hit at the Old Vic. *Teeth* was done on television. And on June 28 it was followed by another half-hour television play, *Another Moon Called Earth* also directed by Alan Gibson and starring John Wood (soon to become the quintessential Stoppard actor).

The significance of this play in the Stoppard canon is obvious. It picks up ideas dealt with in *Lord Malquist and Mr Moon*: it also anticipates, in terms of themes and characters, *Jumpers*. It is a whimsically interesting half-way house. But it seems too slender and fragile a structure to carry all the intellectual cargo loaded on to it: the notion of earthly moral absolutes being thrown into chaos by the idea of moon-landings (still two years away), the question of whether history is a matter of chance events or a grand design, man's curious unwillingness to accept circumstantial evidence when it affects his own sexual security. At his best, Stoppard treats serious issues with cascading lightheartedness. Here he descends into a sketchy playfulness that led one TV reviewer, George Melly, to compare the play unflatteringly to Christopher Fry.

Stoppard picks up on *Lord Malquist* in that his hero, Bone, is not so much a historian as a dissector of the past who seeks to 'lay bare the logic which other men have taken to be an arbitrary sequence of events.' Like his predecessor, Moon, however, he finds the immensity of the task self-defeating: so far he's got as far as the Greeks in the 3rd century BC. What Stoppard seems to be saying is that man has a built-in hunger for pattern and order that the vastness of human knowledge makes it difficult to discern. In contradiction, Arnold Toynbee in *A Study In History* identified 21 civilizations which have passed through similar phases of growth, breakdown and eventual dissolution, the final stage in each case being characterised by the formation of a 'universal state': a dominant minority establishes a temporary peace and within that the proletariat creates a universal church which becomes the chrysalis from which a new civilization eventually emerges. Karl Marx in *Das Kapital* also established universal laws which suggested that capitalism would be superceded by a socialism that would abolish private ownership of the means of production and that the state would eventually wither away as the classless society of Communism approached. Stoppard suggests Bone's task is impossible: history, you might say, proves otherwise.

But Stoppard worries away at the idea of pattern-seeking just as he had done in his novel:

> BONE: . . . You see, I'm not exactly a *historian* – the actual history has all been written up by other people – but I'm discovering the patterns – exposing the fallacy of chance – there are no impulsive acts – nothing random – everything is logical and connects into the grand design.

ALBERT: Is there one?

BONE: There's got to be something going on besides a lot of accidents. If it's all random, then what's the point?

ALBERT: What's the point if it's all logical?

This precisely echoes Moon's belief that behind the simplest action lie a billion connecting moments. It also catches the scepticism of Laura Malquist who wanted to know 'What's the point if it's all inevitable?' I see nothing wrong with Stoppard repeating himself and giving a second airing to important ideas. But whereas *Lord Malquist and Mr Moon* offers a carefully worked-out *demonstration* of the ideas (in the way the casual death of a petitioner in the early pages reverberates in the final ones) in *Another Moon Called Earth* we get a rather airy flotation of Stoppard's themes. A half-hour TV play is simply too lightweight a vehicle to carry such cargo: there is no room to develop the ideas.

Stoppard also carries over from the novel the idea of a desk-bound historian constantly catching his beautiful wife in a series of compromising positions with a man of worldy suavity – in this case, a doctor called Albert – all of which seem to have a perfectly rational explanation. In one sense, this is a variation of a very old joke. I remember a *Playboy* cartoon, at around the same time as the Stoppard play, in which a wife caught *in flagrante* announces to her husband: 'Darling, this is my guru.' There was also a rather feeble 1967 Hollywood film, *A Guide For the Married Man*, in which a wife similarly caught simply pretended her lover didn't exist as he silently put on his clothes and departed. Stoppard does more than wring a few variations on a saloon-bar joke. He implies there is no such thing as objective truth: that any situation can be seen from a number of angles. Bone finds his wife sitting up in bed with Albert kissing her. It may, from one angle, be proof of hanky-panky: it may, from another, be simply a game of phrase-making charades. Stoppard teases the idea out. But again it works rather better in the novel where Moon is driven to distraction by his wife's *trompe l'oeil* promiscuity: here Bone resorts to jokes such as 'My wife's in bed with the doctor at the moment.' Nothing much seems to be at stake.

This play, however, looks forward as well as back. Most clearly, it offers a dry-run for *Jumpers* in that London is staging a ceremonial parade for the return to earth of the first lunanaut – the idea that he might actually be British is rather touching – and in that the heroine, Penelope, believes that the landings on the moon have thrown into question all our earthly assumptions:

PENELOPE: . . . I want to see him – his face – I want to see if it shows, what he has seen.

BONE: What?

PENELOPE: God, is it only me? I tell you, he has stood outside and seen us whole, all in one go, little. And suddenly everything we live by – our rules – our good, our evil – our ideas of love, duty – all the things we've counted on as being absolute truths – because we filled all existence – they're all suddenly exposed as nothing more than local customs – nothing more – Because he has seen the edges where we stop, and we never stopped anywhere before –

BONE: Penelope

PENELOPE: I'm telling you – when that thought drips through to the bottom, people won't just carry on. The things they've taken on trust, they've never had edges before.

I find some big and questionable assumptions here. One is that the moon-landings are as historically important as the discovery of the Copernican theory of the universe in the sixteenth century: indeed Penelope sounds like a medieval churchman wringing his hands over the collapse of the Ptolemaic system. Yet the discovery that the earth was not the centre of the universe but simply part of the inter-planetary system did not disqualify the concepts of good and evil, love and duty; and no more did the lunar landings. Stoppard was actually writing two years or more before the US astronaut, Neil Armstrong, set foot on the fine-grained surface of the moon on July 20, 1969 and you could say he is merely indulging in fanciful speculation. With the benefit of hindsight, it is possible to say that the moon landings produced many diverse reactions: awe at American technology, incredulity at human achievement, anger at the waste of scientific resources, a vague questioning as to whether it was worth all that expenditure of energy to stand on the lifeless, rock-studded surface of the moon. The one thing, for sure, that didn't happen was people standing around questioning moral absolutes. What

Stoppard – and Penelope – overlook is the extent to which television itself deprives a moon-landing of much of its mystery and renders it part of the ceaseless spectacle of public events. TV breeds its own indifference: I can remember how on the night of the actual moon-landing(July 20, 1969) Dennis Norden suggested jokingly that it was probably all a spectacle being staged in a TV studio next door (an idea developed later in a movie, *Capricorn One*). I don't suggest that was the general reaction: merely that, in the age of television, moon-landings, presidential assassinations, spectacular natural disasters become part of the flow of events, that we register them with appropriate reactions and then go out and put the kettle on. Nearly two decades after Stoppard's play, it may be possible to talk about a decline in public standards of behaviour and in a general relaxation of strict moral codes; there are many factors contributing to that. I don't think anyone would sanely argue that a one-shot moon-landing was one of them.

Dramatically, Stoppard also runs up against the problem that the rather frivolous, attention-demanding, seemingly promiscuous Penelope is a rather unlikely vehicle for such abstract speculation about the future of the universe. In the course of the action we also discover that Penelope has thrown her old nanny, Pinkerton, out of a window: ostensibly because Pinkerton kept beating her at games but, in reality, because all the conventional moral laws have been thrown into disarray by the moon-landing. Critics at the time were not slow to point out the improbability of all this. George Melly asked why it took a moon-landing to 'destroy a silly, vain girl's moral sense' and Stanley Reynolds in *The Guardian* wrote: 'Unfortunately Stoppard's brave new moral stance wasn't argued with enough earthbound tribal logic.' That is the real point. Penelope's arguments are uncritically presented as if the mere statement of them made them true; and the murder of old Pinkerton is accepted by everyone with matter-of-fact blandness rather than with the horrific realisation that we may have entered a new moral dimension.

Stoppard's conceits (the man scrabbling to raise a taxi-fare, the voice of the speaking-clock acquiring a human angst) work very well in radio which is a medium primed for fantasy. But there is something about the implacable literalism of television that makes it much harder to contain his 'What if?' ideas.

TV drama is – for better or worse – encased in naturalism and a play like this that sports with far-fetched notions is bound to be diminished by it. For Stoppard-buffs, it has some sprightly dialogue (when Bone claims to be a logician, Albert replies: 'Really? Sawing ladies in half – that kind of thing?') and forms an interesting link in the chain of his development. In the end, however, *Another Moon Called Earth* is a bubble that has been pricked by historical reality and the revelation that the primal human responses and our fundamental moral codes remain intact.

Albert's Bridge

Stoppard's genius for radio emerges very clearly in *Albert's Bridge* which was first transmitted on the Third Programme on July 13, 1967, directed by Charles Lefeaux, and which went on to win the Prix Italia the following year. I would say that part of its quality was that it would defy staging: except that it was presented by the Oxford Theatre Group at Edinburgh in 1969 and at the King's Head in London in 1976. It brings together a lot of Stoppard's by-now abiding themes: the need to get a hold on reality by distancing oneself from it, the overwhelming multiplicity of human existence, the sense of society always poised on the edge of breakdown, the beauties and absurdities of arithmetical logic. All the Stoppard cards are there. So, also, is his recurrent flaw as a writer: a curious detachment from human passions. Stoppard, you feel, creates complex artefacts. But they often seem curiously devoid of real, recognisable people.

The idea behind *Albert's Bridge* is brilliant: one perfectly suited to radio's acoustic virtuosity and ability to handle different planes of reality. We are presented with a four-man team who paint the Clufton Bay Bridge ('the fourth biggest single-span, double-track, shore-to-shore railway bridge in the world') in two-year cycles. A council sub-committee is presented with a new paint that last eight years: it decides to sack three of the painters and let one man do the bridge by himself. The solo volunteer is Albert, a philosophy graduate who shuns a future in his father's firm of Metal Alloys and Allied Metals. Albert's view from the bridge gives him an Olympian perspective on a toy world that only makes sense when one is above it. He becomes obsessed by his work, neglects his wife and child and doesn't even bother to talk down a suicide-case who sees the fundamental precariousness of human order. Albert's perfect world is shattered when the sub-committee realises that, after two years, only one part of the bridge is painted while the other three-quarters is rusty and dilapidated. So, to combat civic disquiet, it despatches 1,800 men to paint the bridge in a single day with the result that the whole structure collapses.

What actually is the play about? I would say it is about two rival, unrealisable dreams of perfection. On the one hand, Albert alone on his bridge sees humanity from a god-like vantage-point and (like Glad, the speaking-clock) appreciates the 'scurrying insignificance' of mortal affairs. Looking down on the university where he studied philosophy, he asks:

'What could they possibly know? I saw more up there in three weeks than those dots did in three years. I saw the context. It reduced philosophy and everything else. I got a perspective. Because that bridge was – separate – complete – removed, defined by principles of engineering which makes it stop at a certain point, which compels a certain shape, certain joints – the whole thing utterly fixed by the rules that make it stay up. It's complete, and a man can give his life to its maintenance, a very fine bargain.'

It is, of course, not such a fine bargain as all that: the price Albert pays is that he sacrifices his family and all social relationships to the majestic harmony of the bridge. And – either listening to or reading the play – it is hard to keep out of one's mind the way distance from humanity often breeds a chilling disregard for the dots on the landscape. Orson Welles's Harry Lime in *The Third Man* has a famous speech in the Ferris-wheel at Vienna's Prater in which he looks at the microscopic ants beneath him with fascistic contempt; and the French literary high-flier, Antoine St Exupery, combined mystical descriptions of the joys of flying with similarly cold-blooded views of the people on the ground. Albert finds a kind of Utopia in solitude, withdrawal and the rhythm of flawless engineering; and in the end he is left asking 'What did I have that they wanted?'

At the other end of the scale, Stoppard satirises the earthbound committee – men who apply fixed rules of mathematical logic and economic constraint to the painting of the bridge. Fitch, the committee's financial wizard, wants to transform the running of a living community to a thing of precision and efficiency, 'a cybernetic poem'. He too is an idealist. But, unfortunately, his plans take the form of a school-examination question:

> 'Gentlemen, let us take as our starting-point the proposition that X painters painting at the rate of Y would take Z years to paint surface ABC. We found that when X equalled four, Z equalled two, Y and ABC remaining constant. Then along came factor P, a paint lasting eight years . . .'

Clearly that way madness lies. And Stoppard shows, very wittily, that you cannot apply inflexible rules to human life. One man taking eight years to paint a bridge is nonsense not only because it leaves the bridge to rust but because it denies the social factors that are part of work: 1,800 men to do the bridge in a day is equal nonsense because it doesn't allow for the stress of human weight. Long before Thatcherism became a force in the land, Stoppard is deftly puncturing the application both of strict logic and of overpowering economic need to the process of work. Albert's dream is unattainable: the committee-men's dessicated logic is unworkable.

What is also impressive is the way Stoppard – in his fourth radio play – uses the medium with masterly freedom. When people talk about 'use of radio' what they often mean is batteries of clangorous sound-effects like the Goon Show gone mad: in fact, the great radio dramatists, such as Giles Cooper, Henry Reed, Don Shaw, Dylan Thomas, Louis Macneice, Samuel Beckett rely on the brilliancy of their dialogue and an ability to leave images resonating in the listener's head. A play like Beckett's *All That Fall* allows us to imagine the ungainly spectacle of the fat Irish woman, Maddy Rooney, being heaved and pushed into Mr Slocum's motor-car like a bale of straw shunted onto a farm-wagon. Radio operates like a private cinema in one's head; but a cinema with the added advantage (one hopes) of good dialogue.

Structurally, *Albert's Bridge* is very like a film; and Stoppard uses his pen as a film-director might his camera. Close-ups of painters doing dip-brush-slap on the bridge, of committee-room wrangles, of Albert being chivvied by his mother or wife alternate with long-shots where we seem to see humanity from Albert's dizzying, vertiginous vantage-point. Even in a single speech Stoppard can go from a distant vision of humanity down to the most intense detail rather like Hitchcock in the opening shot of *Psycho* starting with a comprehensive urban aerial shot and then taking the camera down to one room in one specific hotel hideaway.

ALBERT: Listen . . .
    The Hot sun makes you think of insects,
    but this insect hum is the whole city
    caught in a seashell . . .
    All conversation is hidden there,
    among motors, coughing fits, applause,
    screams, laughter, feet on the stairs,
    secretaries typing to dictation,
    radios delivering the cricket scores,
    tapes running, wheels turning, mills grinding,
    chips frying, lavatories flushing, lovers sighing,
    the mayor blowing his nose.
    All audible life in the vibration
    of a hairdryer in the room below.

This is superb radio writing.

Like all good plays, *Albert's Bridge* works on different levels. It is clearly about two contradictory, unrealisable dreams. I also see in it a fable about the character of the artist himself: a man who, according to Stoppard, has to stand apart from society to make sense of it but who in so doing risks cutting himself off from what gives life to his creation. As we have seen, Stoppard is obsessed in all his early plays by the need for order in human affairs and by the sense that only by detaching oneself from the hurly-burly can one make sense of it. Albert, the philosophical painter, is very like a writer in his total absorption in his task, in his social diffidence and, most specifically, in his feeling that one has to gain a perspective on life that makes sense of it:

ALBERT: Yes, it hits you, when you come back down. How close it all is. You can't stand back to look at it.

I wouldn't push the comparison too far but running through the play is the fear (explored by Ibsen in *When We Dead Awaken*) that the artist sacrifices life to art and ends up with a feeling of cheated disappointment. Albert is, by profession, a bridge-painter but he has the visionary obsessiveness of the artist: his idea of a perfect holiday is a visit to the Firth of Forth and when he goes reluctantly to Paris he spends his time up the Eiffel Tower wondering at the breathtaking pointlessness of it. His wife, Kate, complains: 'You don't talk to me, you don't talk to Katherine, you can't wait to get out of the house and up your favourite girder' exactly like a writer's neglected spouse excoriating the regular retreat to the study.

Just as the writer can only make sense of things through the shaping form of art, so Albert can only get life into perspective by bridge-painting. But Stoppard is also haunted by this strange, personal nightmare that what we take to be the orderly running of society is fragile and precarious and that at any moment the whole structure might fly apart. The suicidal Fraser, who joins Albert on the bridge, expresses this clearly:

> 'I do not believe that there is anyone in control. There is the semblance of pattern – supply meeting demand, one-way streets, give and take, the presumption of return tickets, promises to pay the bearer on demand etcetera – but there's nothing really holding it together. One is forced to recognize the arbitrariness of what we claim to be order. Somewhere there is a lynch-pin which, when removed, will collapse the whole monkey-puzzle.'

Every dramatist maps out his own particular territory. For Harold Pinter, it is the notion that we spend our lives in rooms battling for personal dominance; for Peter Shaffer it is the idea of life as a constant conflict between rational, Appollonian forces and a surging Dionysiac instinct; for Edward Bond it is the idea that the way we organise society crushes our instinctive goodness and harmony and teaches us discord and violence. For Stoppard, in these early plays, it is the concept of life as a battle between random occurrence and a grand design, between chaos and order, between maddening engagement with the multiplicity of things and a retreat into private visions. We have seen that many of his protagonists – Glad, John Brown, Rosencrantz and

60

Guildenstern, Lord Malquist, Mr Moon, Bone, Albert – either hunger for withdrawal or achieve it; and they seem to express a personal need in Stoppard himself for some kind of tactical disengagement from life in order to interpret it. His plays themselves are disciplined, structured, formal, precise, the very antithesis of the displays of raw, personal feeling that motivate a writer like John Osborne. But what one looks for, in vain, are the common human emotions of love, hate, jealousy, private pain or any revelation of what men and women are like when alone. It is interesting that Stoppard sees women in these early plays either as highly-sexed teasers (Jane Moon, Penelope, Mary in *Teeth*) or as long-suffering victims (Persephone in *Enter a Free Man*, Kate in *Albert's Bridge*) of husbands who are prey to some internal demon. They rarely exist in their own independent right.

I started this chapter by discussing Stoppard's first play, originally entitled *A Walk on the Water*. It finally appeared in the West End on March 28, 1968 as *Enter a Free Man* starring Michael Hordern. It was received with the kind of politeness archaeologists might show on digging up a late-Egyptian bracelet after discovering the tomb of Tutankhamun. Irving Wardle in *The Times* wrote: 'Stoppard's most conspicuous gifts are for creating drama from a molecular interplay of ideas and translating abstract speculation into fantastic events. The type of comedy he is meeting here does not give these gifts much of a chance.' Mary Holland in *Plays and Players* more charitably suggested: 'It is concerned with the same big questions as *Rosencrantz and Guildenstern Are Dead* – how does an individual establish and hold on to his identity, how much is any man's identity his own and how much is imposed and changed by circumstances and by people quite outside? Is George Riley right rarely to see and certainly never to admit that he's a failure, always to keep up the belief that the big inventing breakthrough is just around the next corner?' But it is a measure of Stoppard's success in carving out his own territory on the theatrical map that most people now expected something more from him than a mildly funny, healing comedy about a dottily eccentric, impractical dreamer and his long-suffering family. People were now waiting impatiently for Stoppard's next theatrical Catherine wheel.

3

Philosophy and Fireworks

The Real Inspector Hound

They did not have long to wait. On June 17, 1968 Stoppard's *The Real Inspector Hound* opened at the Criterion in a double-bill with Sean Patrick Vincent's *The Audition*, but critical rapture was well-contained. Philip Hope-Wallace in *The Guardian* said 'in total effect it is rather a disappointment and too often facetious.' Peter Lewis in the *Daily Mail* admired the dexterity and ingenuity of Stoppard's jokes while adding 'I couldn't help wishing he had found a bigger theme to exercise them on.' It was left to Ronald Bryden in *The Observer* to enthuse 'As nearly perfect in its kind as a P.G. Wodehouse plot: tiny, ludicrous and beautiful as an ivory Mickey Mouse.' It looks a very slight work. But it has come up very well in a succession of revivals and begins to look like Stoppard's most durable work for the theatre.

Its play-within-a-play format sends my mind spinning back to the greatest of all American critics, George Jean Nathan, who in his *Encyclopedia of Theatre* compiled a list of 25 infallible signs by which a playgoer may know, after the first ten minutes, that he is in the presence of a stinker. I append three of them:

1. If, shortly after the play starts, one of the characters, usually an old woman with a quaver in her voice, shakes her head ominously and remarks with symbolic import there's a storm brewing, whereupon a faint rumble of thunder is heard in the distance.

2. When Annie, the Irish servant-girl, palpitatingly confides to a member of the household: 'A man broke out of the pinitintiary last night and they haven't fond a trace of him yet.'

3. Any mystery play in which, at the very start, someone remarks that the nearest house is two miles away.

Stoppard brings all three of these – and a few more – together in a play that is both a very funny parody of a Christie-esque country-house thriller (it is strangely like *The Mousetrap*) and a study in wish-fulfilment showing how a couple of theatre critics are drawn inexorably into a piece of stage action.

Stoppard begins with a good theatrical image. We, the audience, assemble to see two of our representatives on stage likewise waiting for a play to begin. It so happens they are theatre critics: Birdboot, a plump, vain philanderer who enjoys giving young actresses a leg-up (not to mention a leg-over) and Moon, the perennial second-string irked by the fact that his very presence prompts speculation as to where his Number One is that evening. They find themselves watching a stereotype-thriller complete with radio switched conveniently on to tell us that a suspicious character is at large in the desolate marshes surrounding Muldoon Manor, with a corpse behind the sofa that everyone ostentatiously overlooks and with a comic char who speaks like the stage-directions from a Samuel French acting-edition. One by one the cliché characters assemble: Simon Gascoyne, the rakish juve, Felicity Cunningham, the trim-buttocked ingénue in tennis-gear, Cynthia Lady Muldoon, vivaciously widowed, and Major Magnus, the crippled half-brother of Lord Muldoon who has turned up out of the blue from Canada. We even get Inspector Hound turning up in inflatable pontoons as improbably as the Inspector in *The Mousetrap* arriving at a beleagured snowbound country-house on skis. Events lead up to a second-act curtain in which young Simon is felled by a shot. The third act begins with a phone ringing on an empty stage. Unable to resist the temptation, Birdboot goes to answer it and finds himself drawn into the 'real' world of the play. He finds himself stepping into the shoes of Simon in a replay of the second act and then makes the fatal discovery that the corpse on stage is that of Moon's Number One, Higgs. When Birdboot is shot, Moon himself rushes on stage (Simon and Hound have by now taken over the critics' seats) and becomes implicated in the increasingly frenzied action. He discovers that Major Magnus is both the real Inspector Hound and his own deputy, Puckeridge, who has contrived the deaths of all the others. Moon goes to his death with the words 'Puckeridge . . . you cunning bastard' on his admiring lips.

Now there is an obvious objection to this and it is one that has been frequently made. Clearly Stoppard is bringing two worlds into collision: that of the critics and the play. But, as Irving Wardle pointed out, 'Stoppard's two critics are as unreal as the characters in the thriller ... Stoppard regularly establishes different planes of action and then negates the contrast by showing up every plane as equally unreal. His work is a series of looking-glass adventures: with the difference that his mirrors reflect nothing but themselves. There is no starting point in actuality.'

On a surface level this is true: one does not regularly encounter critical colleagues who come along bearing boxes of chocolates or colour-transparencies of blow-ups of their own notices (there is a limit even to critical vanity). But this is not a Pirandellian play about the world of reality invading that of illusion: it is about two parallel worlds coming into collision. One is a critical world based on a murderous chain-of-succession and on a secret wish to be part of the stage-fantasy setting of bridge, tennis, and lissom young things: the other is the milieu of the stage-thriller likewise rooted in murder and envy. It is also very much a joke about style: about critics who talk like parodies of themselves and about cliché-characters who converse in inverted commas. I confess I did not fully appreciate this until Stoppard himself directed the play in 1985 in a National Theatre double-bill with Sheridan's *The Critic*. Stoppard's production heightened the element of wish-fulfilment in the way Roy Kinnear's Birdboot overcame his first swivel-eyed, panic-stricken look round the stage-set to realise this was the world he had always wanted to be part of and in the way Edward Petherbridge's acidulous, black-leathered Moon began to relish the mechanics of detection once he crossed the footlights. Seeing the play in conjunction with *The Critic* also increased my appreciation of Stoppard's daring. Sheridan's play directly satirises the pretensions of PR men, theatrical hacks and hangers-on and then moves into recreated burlesque: Stoppard interweaves and interlaces two equally idiotic worlds.

Aiming lower than *Rosencrantz and Guildenstern*, *The Real Inspector Hound* hits its target more certainly. As Stoppard himself says, it's not a play about critics: originally he simply had two members of the audience getting drawn into the action. He only chose critics because they're defined and easy to parody. And, having done time himself in the trade, he does pin down certain recognisable qualities. Nathan again said that one of the traps of the job was confusing an aphrodisiac actress with a good one; and Birdboot combines a talent for hyperbolic excess with a panting lechery ('In what is possibly the finest Cynthia since the war –'). Moon is even more identifiable: not only the waspish deputy but the kind of critic who can find eternity in a grain of sand and cosmic significance in the third-rate. It is an old game of critical one-upmanship: to discern hidden meanings in apparently escapist trifles; and Moon plays it as to the manor born:

'Already in the opening stages we note the classic impact of the catalystic figure – the outsider – plunging through to the centre of an ordered world and setting up the disruptions – the shock waves – which unless I am much mistaken will strip these comfortable people – these crustaceans in the rock pool of society – strip them of their shells and leave them exposed as the trembling raw meat which, at heart, is all of us.'

We've all been there. But this is a play about style as much as substance, and Stoppard is equally good at parodying the critical habit of keeping one eye on the stage and another alert for a quotable phrase (my own favourite is 'An uncanny ear that might have belonged to a Van Gogh'). It also harpoons the critical penchant for regarding any work of art as a network of hidden influences as if written by a consensus of literary ghosts. It is not enough that the critics are watching a bad thriller. As Moon shows, it has to be something more:

Faced as we are with such ubiquitous obliquity, it is hard, it is hard indeed, and therefore I will not attempt, to refrain from invoking the names of Kafka, Sartre, Shakespeare, St Paul, Beckett, Birkett, Pinero, Pirandello, Dante and Dorothy L. Sayers.

I suspect it's no accident that four of the names on that list are dramatists who were presumed to have influenced Stoppard in the writing of his previous stage play.

The other half of the equation is the joke-thriller confronting the critics; and what has been little noticed here is the way Stoppard parodies a bad play while actually managing to write a good one. Once again it is very much a style joke with characters talking like walking stage-directions. Thus Mrs Drudge says into the phone: 'Hello, the drawing-room of Lady Muldoon's country residence one morning in early spring.' (I am reminded of the true story told me by a County Drama Adviser who once came upon an amateur production of a blameless comedy in which he was surprised to find, amidst the banter, an actor delivering all his lines while squatting underneath a table. Puzzled by this unwarranted touch of Ionesco in what was a light drawing-room comedy he enquired of the director what this portended. She told him it was all in the stage-direction which announced 'Enter Frederick who crosses down left and sits below table.'). Stoppard also catches perfectly the kind of thriller-chat that is loaded with double-meanings that come up and hit you sharply between the shoulder-blades. Simon has absented himself from Felicity a while to make love to Cynthia: a point duly made under the pontoon-bridge:

CYNTHIA: Did I hear you say you saw Felicity last night, Simon?
SIMON: Did I? – Ah yes, yes, quite – your turn, Felicity.
FELICITY: I've had my turn, haven't I Simon? – now, it seems, it's Cynthia's turn.
CYNTHIA: That's my trick, Felicity dear.

All the stigmata of the stinky thriller are here: the cut-off house, the maniac on the loose, the overlooked corpse, the carefully overheard, incriminating remarks giving everyone that moves a motive and a cue for murder. But Stoppard also piles on the sight-gags as his own expertly-staged production reminded us: Jonathan Hyde as Major Magnus Muldoon zoomed down a flight of stairs in a wheelchair like a runaway cripple, Ian McKellen as Inspector Hound arrived with what looked like two Dunlop tyres strapped to his feet and vainly admired himself in the mirror he had used to establish a suspect's expiry and, best of all, Selina Cadell as Mrs Drudge hobbled across the stage with agonising arthritic slowness as she poured out four cups of coffee in painful succession.

But what is fascinating about the thriller side of the play is that it is interwoven with the parody-critic side to make a kind of logical sense. Stoppard has said that when he began writing he had no idea that the body was going to be Higgs or that Magnus was going to be Puckeridge. Yet when Moon's gorge rises in protest at the question 'Where's Higgs?' he cries: 'The very sight of me with a complimentary ticket is enough. The streets are impassable tonight, the country is rising and the cry goes up from hill to hill – Where-is-Higgs? (*Small pause.*) Perhaps he's dead at last . . .' Yes indeed. And having elected to draw Birdboot into the action, Stoppard plausibly shows how his nocturnal dalliance with the actress playing Felicity and his sudden, unconquerable passion for the one playing Cynthia enables him to step easily into the shoes of Simon Gascoyne who is himself involved with both women: all part of the Chinese puzzle effect that makes a fiendishly well-constructed play out of a parody of a bad one. The critic plot and the thriller plot begin to coincide like a carefully-etched tracing laid on top of an original drawing. So much so that when we come to the final explanations and a parody of one of those plot-unravelling Christie denouements that no-one ever fully understands, we find that Gascoyne and Birdboot have become so inextricably merged that the words applied to one equally well fit the other:

> MOON: Gascoyne bided his time but in due course tracked McCoy down to this house having, on the way, met in the neighbourhood, a simple ambitious girl from the provinces. He was charming, persuasive – told her, I have no doubt, that she would go straight to the top – and she, flattered by his sophistication, taken in by his promises to see her all right on the night, gave in to his simple desires.

Stoppard has said that he wanted a plot that would resolve itself in a breathtakingly neat, complex but utterly comprehensible way; and so it does with the revelation that Puckeridge (established early on as a wan shadow of a shadow, a stand-in's stand-in) is the vengeful murderer *and* the disguised detective *and* the amnesiac husband of Lady Muldoon. It is as if *The Mousetrap* had been re-written by Ionesco; and it says a lot for the play's deftness that Birdboot spotted early on that Magnus/Puckeridge/Inspector Hound was the murderer.

This is a well-made play with neither spare flesh nor loose

ends. As Helen Dawson wrote in *Plays and Players*, 'In an age of earnest Happenings and the cult of the improvised Stoppard is courageous enough to continue to cultivate the reactionary talents of the craftsman.' It is a fair point since 1968 was the year that saw not only improvisation and Happenings but the demise of the Lord Chamberlain and a good many evenings revealing both spare flesh and loose ends. London heard a lot of the four-letter word, rejoiced in cunnilingus in *The Beard*, two gays having a baby in *Spitting Image*, prison sodomy in *Fortune and Men's Eyes*, pot smoked and pots disclosed in *Hair*. It was, according to taste, a time of taboo-smashing liberation or an anything-goes descent into anarchy. What is interesting is that Stoppard's lightly-regarded *jeu d'esprit* has survived in the repertory rather better than the more acclaimed, serious plays of the year: *The Hotel in Amsterdam*, *The Ruling Class*, *The Apprentices*. One reason is that craftmanship gets it revenge in the long run, but it is also because Stoppard's play is actually about something eternally true. Like *Rosencrantz and Guildenstern*, it is about two outsiders drawn into a puzzling, confused, murder-story which they only half-understand and which leads ultimately to their deaths. Where the former play is flawed by an academic pretentiousness, however, this one is about the subtle relationship between players and spectators and about the secret desire they often entertain to change ends. Critics often suffer from what Grotowski once called an 'impotence-complex' as they sit nightly watching other people re-create life, but the paying customer too often wonders what it would be like to be drawn into the action on stage. Stoppard takes this common fantasy and, with rigorous logic, follows it through to a nightmare conclusion. That is why *The Real Inspector Hound* will last as long as the stage and the auditorium remains, from our side, one of the great uncrossable frontiers.

Neutral Ground

Spy-fiction was one of the dominant literary forms of the 1960s: suddenly John le Carré and Len Deighton became required reading. Why exactly? Partly because of the vogue for the anti-hero; partly because in the spy we found an image of the way social and political pressures erode individual autonomy: the free agent invariably turned out to be a pawn in someone else's game and exposed the moral bankruptcy of both East and West. Eric Ambler and Graham Greene had explored such territory in the 1940s, but the genre found a master in John le Carré who combined a detailed knowledge of the workings of intelligence agencies with a disillusioned realism that perfectly fitted the spirit of the times.

Given that, it is odd to find Stoppard offering such an apologetic Introduction to his TV play, *Neutral Ground*, which was transmitted by Granada in December, 1968, with Patrick Magee and Nicholas Pennell, though written some three years earlier. Stoppard explains that it was intended to be part of a series based on myths and legends and that he based the piece on the *Philoctetes* of Sophocles with a little help from Euripides. 'I hustled my way,' says Stoppard, 'into a commission, selling the potency of the Philoctetes myth and then concocting a plot out of Sophocles and John le Carré. The series never happened because not enough of the commissioned plays found favour. Three years later *Neutral Ground* was taken off the shelf and produced, somewhat to my dismay, as a single play, the only vestige of the series idea being the hero's egregious name of Philo.' Such defensiveness is needless. The play is a very ingenious adaptation of the original story. It shows Stoppard can write a straight narrative that holds the attention. It also contains signs of Stoppard's own detestation of Soviet imperialism as well as suggestions that the defence of democracy requires indulgence in dirty-tricks. A genre-piece it may be; but Stoppard puts something of himself into it and, for the first time, writes about the public world.

He has the advantage of one of the great classical masterpieces as his springboard. Sophocles's play is set on the desert island of Lemnos where Philoctetes, struck down by disease, was abandoned by his fellow-Greeks on their way to lay siege to Troy. Ten years later Odysseus comes to bring him to Troy because of a prophecy that only Philoctetes, with the bow and arrows of Heracles, can take the city. Odysseus knows that his pleas won't work. So he brings with him Neoptolemus, the young son of Achilles, whose job is to deceive Philoctetes and lure him aboard ship. Neoptolemus wins Philoctetes's confidence with a false story of his quarrel with the Greek commanders, acquires the bow but is moved to pity by the crippled hero's misfortunes. He reveals the deception, eventually restores the bow to its owner but tries to persuade Philoctetes that, for his own good, he must go to Troy. He fails and is asked to fulfil his original promise to take Philoctetes home which will mean the renunciation of his own martial ambitions. Only a divine intervention by Heracles saves the situation and the play ends happily with the hero leaving for a taste of Trojan glory. As Maurice Bowra pointed out, the Sophoclean irony is that the experienced stratagems of Odysseus are shown to be wanting 'and all the assumptions on which the play begins are destroyed by the emergence of truth in words and feelings.'

Stoppard takes this story, gives it a modern setting and imbues it with a modern cynicism about the personal betrayals required by the defence of freedom. What is good is that he allows the moral attitude to emerge from the story and denies himself any of those dazzling, virtuoso set-pieces that have become his personal signature. John Russell Taylor, reviewing the original production, found it 'just a very routine addition to the cycle of downbeat, John le Carré spy dramas.' But I find the lack of hectic self-advertisement and punning cleverness right for the story; and even without that a quick eye can still detect traces of Stoppard's private feelings.

Stoppard's hero, Philo, is an East European agent whose country has been swallowed up by the Russians and who has been passing secrets to the British. He makes a break for it but on arrival in the West is virtually discarded by Otis (Odysseus), a hard-headed American who has replaced an old British buffer as head of the espionage network. Philo retreats into drunken bitterness in a village in the fictive small country of Montebianca and decides to await death. Some time later Otis decides he needs Philo again to decode new information on 'the Reschev case' (never properly defined) and so a young British agent, Acherson (Achilles son), is despatched to Philo's village in the guise of a salesman to surreptitiously winkle him out. At the same time a couple of Soviet bloc heavies, Laurel and Hardy, are also hot on Philo's trail. Rather as in Sophocles's play, Acherson pretends to be disillusioned with his own masters to win Philo's confidence. He does so but, at the very last moment, he blows the whole strategy and warns Philo that once he steps on the train he thinks he is returning him to his native-land he will be appropriated by the West. Realising that Acherson has risked his future for his sake, Philo boards the train. But the final shot

shot suggests that Acherson has been playing a game of double-bluff and is filled with self-disgust.

There is minor academic sport to be had watching the way Stoppard plunders classical myth. Philoctetes was physically diseased: Philo is a moral leper initially unwanted by the West and unable to return to the East. Odyssean deceit and Achillean truthfulness are represented by Otis's brutal pragmatism and Acherson's distaste for his task. Even the code-name that is used for the Western operation – Toytown, supposedly referring to an international toy-company – is a modern variation of Troy town. Having set up the parallels Stoppard also uses them. Frontier railway stations provide a visual motif. When Philo defects he and Otis conduct their barbed dialogue in a Toytown store-room while playing with a toy train set, with Otis skilfully working the points until a duff British agent causes a derailment. Stoppard's love of craft meshes well with the dynamics of the spy story.

This lifts the play above routine. So, too, does Stoppard's ability to invest the characters with some emotional dynamic. I have complained about Stoppard's previous inability to recognise that the heart is as powerful an organ as the brain: I have often felt poor Tom's a cold, but a genre piece like this, paradoxically, permits him some emotional licence. Stoppard, now a fervent Englishman, often describes himself as 'a bounced Czech' and he gives Philo the anger of the refugee from a ruthlessly colonised country:

OTIS: Why did you have enough?
PHILO: Look, I wasn't in it for your country. I had my own.
OTIS: Common interest.
PHILO: That may have been so in the old days. Now my country doesn't even show on *your* maps. The tanks have been followed by the map-makers, and in the schools the children are only taught Russian. I wasn't doing any good in there. I was doing more before.

Stoppard has always been fascinated by people caught between conflicting moral positions. Here he turns his attention to someone caught between conflicting political ideologies and occupying the neutral ground of the title: as Philo says 'I'm a used-up spy without a country and I'm asking you to recognise

71

me.' This may not be a profound statement but the piece does deal graphically with the pathos of exile and with the disregard for the individual shown by inflexible systems.

Stoppard presses home the point through Acherson who is a decent English public-school type involved in a business now run by multi-national committees. His job is to get through to Philo by expressing his distaste for his masters and the whole beastly game, but the point of the play is that his assumed feelings become his real ones. The mask becomes the face:

> 'They're making a scapegoat out of me, old man. Acherson pays so that honour is satisfied and the big chief can carry on. Well, he's probably right. And furthermore I don't care because it was making me sick – the callous abstraction of human lives: the pin moved across the map, the card removed from the index . . . it's a trick, old man, a sleight of hand which allows the occasional squalid alliance for the necessary end, the exceptional act of injustice for the overall good, the regrettable sacrifice for the majority's health – yes he's probably right and he's certainly got the cleanest nose in Christendom but if there's a God above it will catch up on him one day and perhaps he will see himself as the cold-blooded zombie he really is, and I wish to God I could be there.

W.H. Auden once wrote a famous essay – 'The Guilty Vicarage' – in which he compared the detective-story to Greek tragedy and said its interest lay in 'the dialectic of innocence and guilt'. The great advantage of genre-fiction and movies is that they allow for a discussion of ethical issues within the framework of popular entertainment. A film like *High Noon* is no less about the conflict between love and duty than a tragedy by Corneille. The Florida-based private-investigator stories of John D. Macdonald deal with individual honour in a society fuelled by rapacity and greed. The great Chandler once described the fictional private eye as a man 'who is neither tarnished nor afraid' giving him a moral dimension most authors would be loath to attach to their heroes. The great advantage of the spy-thriller is that it places the individual against the background of a political system, and suggests that both West and East employ similar means for vastly different ends. It's escapist; but the stories of Burgess, Maclean, Blunt and Philby suggest that the escape is into something approximating to real life.

Stoppard capitalises on all this in *Neutral Ground* in much the same way Harold Pinter did in scripting *The Quiller Memorandum* (his best work for the cinema). There is also a crucial Pinter parallel in the idea of a beleaguered hero hiding away in an inaccessible spot and being pursued by two roguishly jocular killers: *The Birthday Party* goes to Montebianca. But Stoppard's far from negligible script also works because it has just the right amount of eccentric detail and thriller-tension. The killers are combing Montebianca looking for Philo. The one clue they have to go on is his attachment to a pet-monkey. They strong-arm a vet to let them know who in town has such a creature. They are given the name of Buchner and, certain they have their man, they burst in on a woman in a négligé eating breakfast off a tray and feeding soft-boiled egg to her pet monkey. Later the still-pursuant Laurel and Hardy catch up with Acherson and raid his car only to find it full of toy six-shooters and dolls. At first, they think it's the wrong car. They then realise it is Acherson's, make him get in it and drive out to the country with the obvious intention of killing or torturing him. As the Fiat draws up at a lonely spot, Acherson picks up a toy Lone Ranger gun and shoots his ambushers dead.

This may not seem the height of dramatic art, but a well-plotted thriller requires more craft than a personal-statement play. Stoppard uses the format to expose the loneliness of those who occupy neutral ground and the shabby, amoral compromises of those whose job it is to protect our freedom. The supposed strait-jacket of the genre proves strangely liberating; and, almost for the first time in one of his plays, Stoppard makes us care about the people.

Where Are They Now?

One of the surprising – and commendable – things about Stoppard is his willingness to accept small commissions in between the larger ones: in that sense, he is a jobbing dramatist in much the same way that he was a jobbing journalist. After a relatively quiet 18 months following the staging of *The Real Inspector Hound* – during which he was involved in the American production of *Rosencrantz and Guildenstern* and the expansion of *The Dissolution of Dominic Boot* into a mini-film called *The Engagement* – he quietly re-emerged in January,

1970 with a 35-minute play for BBC Schools Radio, *Where Are They Now?*, that earned him precisely £75. It may not be major Stoppard; but it is a deft comedy intercutting between a school dinner in 1945 and an Old Boys' dinner in 1969 and it has touches of true feeling in its account of the way the happiness of childhood is eroded by fear. Stoppard is often praised for his idiosyncratic brilliance, attacked when he writes like other men. I think it is good to be reminded that he can – when he wishes – deal with common, familiar sentiments.

Stoppard, who attended a public school in Pocklington, Yorkshire from 1948 to 1954, is hardly the first English writer to observe that public-school products are stained by their experiences for the rest of their days; nor will he be the last. Cyril Connolly pinned down a truth when he wrote: 'The experiences undergone by boys at the great public schools, their glories and disappointments, are so intense as to dominate their lives and to arrest their development. From these it results that the greater part of the ruling class remains adolescent, school-minded, self-conscious, cowardly, sentimental and, in the last analysis, homosexual.' George Macbeth, in his savagely brilliant poem *The Cleaver Garden*, goes further and sees the militaristic, Empire-building tendency of the British as something nourished by the public-school system. He quotes a British officer, writing home after the battle of the Somme, who said: 'I've known nothing to equal this since I was at Winchester.' And one of Macbeth's stanzas runs:

> Bullying starts things. It can rent
> A premise in the ringworm. What was meant
> As a light-headed romp ends up a tournament.
>
> The whistle blows. All sanctions fail
> And Eton is as bad as Passchedaele.
> The pederastic shell-bursts blossom. Frankly male
>
> You may be, but forced running yields
> Female physiques. Boys start from Furness Fields
> Cross-country through the mud they flounder for steel shields.
>
> Life is a battle. School is war
> And heroes are begotten by that roar.
> Listen. The dying lions yell for more and more.

Stoppard's play is less fierce and explicit than that, but it does say clearly enough that school misshapes, as well as shapes, our characters and that its petty tyrannies and fears linger on.

Stoppard's school dinner takes place in wartime 1945 and is dominated by nicknames, slang, jokes, punishment, irony and the unspoken sense of belonging to an élite fraternity. The boy serving dinner is 'on tucker', anyone genuinely ill gets a 'mog chit' and is sent to 'Staggers' but if it is thought you are malingering you are put on 'tunky' for a whole weekend. The Latin master, Dobson – as much a prisoner of this world as the boys – presides over the proceedings jocularly bullying the 13-year-old pupils into giving him the Latin root of words and exploiting that thinly-veiled sarcasm that most teachers wear like an extra skin. When one boy cries (I should say 'blubs') at the prospect of an encounter with the sadistic French master, Dobson's response is: 'You really shouldn't get into such a state over Mr Jenkins. He no doubt has a thankless task trying to educate you in a subject that will prove invaluable to you in later life should you join the Foreign Legion, which most of you will probably have to . . .' This is not Dotheboys Hall, but it is a horribly accurate recreation of that world of facetiousness and terror over small things that many of us are heir to. The boys respond by forming their own protective groups: the central trio at the 1945 dinner are Groucho, Chico and Harpo.

Stoppard inter-cuts that world with an Old Boys' Reunion in 1969. Dobson is still there like some built-in part of the fabric. Groucho, who used to get Mexican honey sent by his mother from Mexico, is now Marks, a vulgarly affluent businessman throwing out casual boasts about his silver. Chico, who was rather more restrained, is now an indigent, verbally precise vicar. Harpo, who at school was appropriately silent and who went in terror of the French master, is now a crusading journalist who bears the hurts of schooldays like stigmata. School has, in every sense, formed their characters. But the absurd clannishness of such occasions is highlighted by the presence of a guest called Jenkins who gets all the references wrong and who turns out to have strayed into the wrong reunion.

Stoppard links the world of past and present partly by technical devices – the conjugation of the Latin verb 'to laugh' leads directly into a scene where a grown-up guest is rebuked for an unseemly guffaw – but much more by a sense of recollected pain. The crisis in the play comes when the Old Boys are asked to stand in memory of the recently-deceased French master, Mr Jenkins. Gale, 'Harpo', who has come to the dinner specially to see if there are some other dimensions to his old tormentor he never discovered, ostentatiously refuses to stand. And when told by his neighbour at dinner (who actually wasn't at the school) that some people have happier memories of the past, Gale unleashes a speech that is rare in Stoppard for its sense of personal agony:

> GALE: Oh yes, the snows of yesteryear . . . Where were they *then*? Oh, where the Fat Owl of the Remove, where the incorruptible Steerforth? Where the Harrow match and your best friend's beribboned sister? Whither Mr Chips? Oh no, it's farewell to the radiators and the punishable whisper, cheerio to the uncomprehending trudge through *Macbeth* and sunbeams defined by chalkdust, the sense of loss in the fruitcake sent from home, the counted days, the hollow fear of inconsiderable matters, the hand raised in bluff – *Sir, sir, me sir*.

I find this very touching. It contrasts the dream-image of public-school life with the reality and in a few evocative phrases conjures up the past precisely. 'Sunbeams defined by chalkdust' is a beautiful image for light filtering through dark Victorian classrooms on sunny afternoons in a chalky funnel; and 'the hollow fear of inconsiderable matters' pinpoints exactly the disproportion of school-life where minor crises are magnified into major traumas: where a French lesson can become a source of nightmarish terror. Gale goes on to say that childhood is 'Last Chance Gulch for happiness' and that to diminish that happiness through wanton cruelty is a sin. The unspoken irony, of course, is that Gale's later success as a campaigning journalist has clearly been influenced by his dislike of the arbitrary terror of school life.

Stoppard, as we have seen, does not often take a stand or imbue his work with much emotion. But here he leaves us in no doubt that public-school life marks our characters for ever. And lest we delude ourselves into thinking all has changed Stoppard includes a scene where Marks's son is dubbed 'wet', 'stinky' and a 'moronic little tick' for calling a prefect by his nickname and is soundly thumped. This is a little-known Stoppard play but a very good one: it has a just, measured indignation at the injuries inflicted on us by school and at the way the happiness to which childhood is due is chipped and tarnished by fear.

After Magritte

I have praised Stoppard's craftsmanship but his delight in the well-made artefact can also lead him into a rather mechanical approach to drama in which everything is as rigidly patterned and organised as a crossword puzzle. That is what you find in *After Magritte* which was written as a 40-minute squib for the Ambiance Lunch-Hour Theatre Club (where it was first played in April 1970) and which was subsequently seen, both in London and New York, as a curtain-raiser to *The Real Inspector Hound*. For me this is Stoppard at his most tiresome: arch, clever-clever and organising his ideas into an over-neat pattern. I believe in the well-made play but that is not so much a matter of tying everything up in a neat bundle as observing a proper sense of rhythm and proportion: in that sense, *Waiting for Godot* and *The Chairs* are as much well-made plays as anything by Rattigan or Pinero. But the best drama has about it also something of the mysterious, inexplicable and arbitrary (like life itself). It is not simply an Acrostic to be solved.

Stoppard's *After Magritte* is based on a straightforward proposition: that behind the most bizarre, unlikely, surreal image there is often a logical explanation. He has also revealed in interviews that the play had a starting-point in fact. 'Somebody I know had a couple of peacocks in the garden and one escaped while he was shaving. He chased it and had to cross a main road to catch it, and he was standing in his pyjamas with shaving cream on his face holding a peacock when the traffic started going by. This was one of those moments when somebody tells you something and you realize that in due course it's going to be useable, so I built it up forwards and backwards between the first image and the last image.'

Stoppard also told a Dutch interviewer that the play stemmed from a liking for Magritte: for his combination of absurdist humour and the ability to make things very carefully and perfectly. The play, however, is actually a denial of everything Magritte stood for: it uncovers the rational explanation for surreal images. Magritte's paintings take the form of a dialogue with the world and are intended to make us look at and question the reality of real phenomena. In his 1949 manifesto, *Le Vrai Art de la Peinture*, Magritte wrote: 'The perfect painting produces an immense effect only for a very short time and emotions resembling the first emotion felt are to a greater or lesser extent soiled by habit . . . The true art of painting is to conceive and realise paintings capable of giving the spectator a pure visual perception of the external world.' Magritte's paintings are exercises in seeing: they make us aware, by contradiction, of the appearance of a sky, a pipe, a woman. 'This is not a pipe', Magritte writes under a banal painting of a pipe. And in a painting like *Personal Values* he presents us with magnified versions of a comb, a glass, a bar of soap, a shaving-brush, a pencil to make us aware of the puzzling oddity, and even menace, of the everyday. He is not saying there is a simple, rational explanation for everything: he is forcing us to look afresh at the real world.

Stoppard's play, however is Magritte tamed for the tidy-minded. He provides us with a set of frantically odd images and then shows there is a mundane, logical explanation for them. Thus at curtain-rise he presents us with an old woman lying on an ironing-board with one foot propped up against the flat of an iron with her head and part of her face concealed in a tight-fitting black rubber bathing-cap and a black bowler-hat reposing on her stomach. There is also a younger woman in a full-length ballgown who is discovered on her hands and knees staring at the floor ahead. And there is a man with bare torso, evening-dress trousers and fishing waders with his head tilted back as he blows in the recesses of a lampshade. The head of a police-constable, looking like a cut-out, is seen gazing through the window at this extraordinary scene.

It transpires that the old woman is lying prone on the ironing-board because of a bad back, that the woman in the ballgown has been preparing herself for a competition at the North Circular Dancerama and is on the floor looking for lead slugs from a .22 calibre pistol that fill a porcelain container that acts as counterweight to the light-fitting, and that her husband, while waiting for his dress-shirt to be ironed, is meanwhile trying to cool a hot bulb before removing it with his fingers and is wearing waders to keep his black, patent leather shoes clean.

Once that has been made clear, much of the play's action hinges on what the family (Harris, Thelma and the tuba-playing Mother – whose mother no-one is quite sure) exactly saw on their way out of a Magritte exhibition at the Tate Gallery. Harris is convinced he saw an old man with one leg and a white beard, dressed in pyjamas, hopping along in the rain with a tortoise under his arm and brandishing a white stick. Thelma is equally convinced that what she saw was a one-legged footballer in West Bromwich Albion colours with shaving-foam on his face and maybe a football or a wineskin or a pair of bagpipes under his arm and swinging a white stick in the form of an ivory cane. Mother is not much help either: she thinks she saw an escaped convict in striped prison uniform carrying a crocodile-skin handbag under his arm.

To add to the complexity the house is invaded by a demented policeman, Chief Inspector Foot ('Not Foot of the Yard,' cries Harris) who believes the Harrises are involved in a postulated robbery involving a one-legged, black-faced minstrel; and Mother is a devotee of the tuba who has insisted on being taken to the Magritte exhibition but who has been disappointed by his unrealistic representation of the instruments and rather doubts if he ever tried to play one. In the end all the various oddities are explained and the bizarre image seen by the family after the Magritte show was none other than Inspector Foot who, in order to secure a parking-meter dashed out of the house in the middle of shaving, grabbed his wife's handbag for the small change and her parasol to keep off the rain and thrust both feet into the leg of his pyjama trousers. As Harris says: 'There is obviously a perfectly logical explanation for everything.'

We roughly agree on what is tragedy: comedy is a matter of taste. And there may be those who find this play a source of unbuttoned hilarity. It does – for me – have the odd funny exchange:

THELMA: My legs are insured for £5,000.
HARRIS: Only against theft.

It also has quite a few lines that have nothing to do with the character but a lot to do with the author: 'I never took semaphor as a sophomore, morse the pity,' says Harris with excruciating improbability.

What knocks the play on the head for me is that Stoppard never really rejoices in the absurd irrational humour for its own sake or delights in the oddities of family life in the manner of N.F. Simpson in his unforgettably entitled comedies *A Resounding Tinkle* and *One Way Pendulum*. Simpson rides his own anarchic instinct letting it take him where it will. Thus in the former play Bro and Middie Paradock, a quiet suburban couple, are disturbed by the presence of an elephant they had not ordered in their front garden and are not sure how to name it. Middie favours 'Mr Trench' while Bro goes for something a little more dashing like ''Tis-Pity-She's-A-Whore-Hignett.' Simpson, in Tynan's phrase, celebrates 'the glorious uniqueness of everything that is.' Stoppard is more orderly, and consequently he misses some of the fun of the arbitrary, the accidental, the unforeseen, the irrelevant which often gives life to drama. It would be unfair to hammer this particular play which was never intended as more than a lunchtime *divertissement*, but it does reinforce a general point about Stoppard which is that he often subordinates his characters to a grand design and rarely allows them to go off in totally unexpected directions.

Dogg's Our Pet

This was an occasional piece written for the opening of Inter-Action's Almost Free Theatre in Soho in December, 1971. Inter-Action, a co-operative organisation devoted both to the dissemination of drama and community work was the brainchild of a cigar-chomping American, Ed Berman. The production of plays was only one part of the group's admirable work and that was entrusted to Dogg's Troupe, so named after the pseudonym Berman had invented for himself in case he should ever turn to the production of rhyming verse for children – Dogg. R.L. Out of that labyrinthine whimsy Stoppard wrote an opening-play, *Dogg's Our Pet*, an anagram of Dogg's Troupe, which manages at the same time to be a daffy parody of a regally-attended and stiffly-formal opening ceremony, and an extended linguistic joke based on Wittgenstein (whom Stoppard had clearly been reading as his mental gymnastic work in preparation for *Jumpers*). I will consider the play in the more elaborate revised version *Dogg's Hamlet* that appeared eight years later.

A few points, however, are worth making. In a very short play, no more than 25-minutes long, Stoppard manages to work on two levels. You can take the play simply as a wry farce in which a workman mutinously constructs a platform out of planks, bricks and cubes hurled at him from the wings and in which a superior royal personage formally cuts a ribbon and announces 'Sod the pudding club.' Or you can take it as a theatricalisation of Wittgenstein's *Tractatus* which argues that language, if it is to have a definite meaning, must contain propositions that are pictures of the facts of which the world is composed. Stoppard takes this further by showing us a workman calling out 'Plank', 'Slab', 'Block', 'Brick', 'Cube' and receiving the appropriate pieces. He then posits the idea that, if the second man knew in advance which pieces Charlie needed and in what order, those self same words might constitute an alternative language in which the words translated as 'Here', 'Ready', 'Next', 'The thrower's name' and 'Thank You'. If life consisted simply of building platforms, the two men could go on almost indefinitely without realising they were using words with totally different meanings. Complications would only arise when a third person entered using language in a way puzzling both to Charlie and to Brick.

Dogg's Our Pet is a slight, amusing piece. This is theatre almost as an improvisatory game: indeed the play corresponds to a familiar actors' exercise in which the content of a scene has to be conveyed through unintelligible gibberish. It shows, however, Stoppard's ability to work on two levels and is a harbinger of his increasing fascination with the relativity not merely of concepts but of words themselves and of their ability to take on different meaning depending on the context in which they are used.

Jumpers

The first night of Stoppard's *Jumpers* at the Old Vic on February 2, 1972 was a major theatrical event. It had been nearly five years since his first full-length play established his critical and popular success. In the interim there had been radio and television plays and a number of one-actors but a questionmark still hung over him. Was he a blazing comet or a permanent star in our theatrical firmament? *Jumpers* proved beyond doubt his brilliance, his daring, his determination to extend the possibilities of the stage: here was a British dramatist writing, for heaven's sake, a philosophic farce and assuming an audience could keep up with a fairly intricate debate between academics who believe in absolute values and those who are moral relativists. Over the years I have read and re-read the play and seen other productions (Peter Wood's revival at the Lyttelton in 1976, Nicholas Hytner's version at the Manchester Royal Exchange in 1984, Peter Wood's West End production at the Aldwych in 1985) and occasional doubts have begun to creep in. But it would be dishonest to deny the breath-taking impact *Jumpers* makes when one first sees it in the theatre.

To anyone familiar with *Lord Malquist and Mr Moon* and *Another Moon Called Earth*, the ideas around which the play revolves are not new. *Jumpers* was clearly the result of several years of trial-and-error as well as reading and research (I have an indelible memory of meeting Stoppard on the steps of the London Library laden with books some time before *Jumpers* opened. 'What have you got there?' I innocently asked. 'My next play', he crisply replied). Stoppard goes into training for a new, major play like Daley Thompson preparing for the Decathlon.

What Stoppard has taken from his own novel and TV plays is first of all a fundamental, ungovernable concern about the nature of moral sanctions. The impotent historian Moon, in *Lord Malquist and Mr Moon*, puts it thus:

'I cannot commit myself to either side of a question. Because if you attach yourself to one or the other you disappear into it. And I can't even side with the balance of morality because I don't know whether morality is just an instinct or an imposition.'

Stoppard himself in defining what *Jumpers* was about put it very similarly: 'whether social morality is simply a conditioned response to history and environment or whether moral sanctions obey an absolute, intuitive, God-given law.' Stoppard inherited more than just this from his seminal, unjustly neglected novel. In the book, Moon suffers a good deal of torment through his wife's equivocal involvement (do they do it or don't they?) with a stylish, aristocratic figure on whom he is economically dependent: in the play the moral philosopher, George Moore, goes through

82

similar anguish because of his wife's seeming-dalliance with the omnicompetent University Vice-Chancellor, Archie. In the novel, the private events take place against a background of a spectacular national funeral: in the play there is a similar feeling of a historical turning-point with the assumption to power of the anti-democratic Radical-Liberal Party and the images of a British astronaut condemning a colleague to extinction on the surface of the moon. But the striking thing about the novel is its ability to combine serious ideas with a gaudy, madcap concatention of events. What Stoppard has done in *Jumpers* is to translate that combination of the supposedly irreconcileable – the serious and the comic – into extravagant theatrical terms.

It is worth talking about the other influences on *Jumpers* because they are many and diverse: they range from the groves of academe to the grotesqueries of showbiz. At the heart of the play is an attempt by George Moore to compose a lecture on the existence (or otherwise) of God and the nature of moral absolutes, while in a neighbouring-room his disintegrating, ex-showbiz wife Dotty attempts to dispose of a corpse: the body, in fact, of a logical positivist and practising gymnast who has been shot in the first scene at one of Dotty's parties.

Stoppard is obviously calling on a whole tradition of twentieth-century philosophical debate. The hero's namesake George Moore (1873-1958) was a contemporary of Bertrand Russell's whose most famous work, *Principia Ethica*, written when he was 30, championed the faculty of direct moral awareness and claimed to discover that affectionate personal relations and the contemplation of beauty are the only supremely good states of mind: ideas that had a big influence on Bloomsbury. Moore also believed that when common sense came into conflict with philosophy it was wrong and he spent much time demolishing the ideas of his old teacher McTaggart (interesting that McFee is the name of the murdered positivist) that time is unreal. Moore was the product of a native, empiricist tradition that went back to Locke, Hume and Mill and found fulfilment in the works of both himself and Bertrand Russell. But Moore's moral and religious affirmations were questioned both by Russell and by A.J. Ayer whose central tenet was that for an utterance to be meaningful it must be verifiable either by sense experience or by scrutiny of the conventions governing its use of terms: utterances that were neither empirical nor analytic were at best expressions of feeling. A.J. Ayer was wittily despatched by the *Sunday Times* to cover Stoppard's play at the Old Vic and lucidly pinned down its theme: 'The argument is between those who believe in absolute values, for which they seek a religious sanction, and those, more frequently to be found among contemporary philosophers, who are subjectivists or relativists in morals, utilitarians in politics and atheists or at least agnostics.' Stoppard also draws on the psychological school of Behaviourism – and in particular the ideas of the American psychologist B.F. Skinner – which studies only observable, and preferably measurable, behaviour and leaves out of account consciousness or introspection.

Stoppard clearly did his homework, and there are many other sources at work on the play. One of the least-noticed, although Stoppard acknowledges it in a footnote to the text, is a brilliant French revue, *La Plume de ma Tante* by Robert Dhery, which played at the Garrick in 1955. I have an indelible memory of a sketch in which a girl on a swing sings a number from *Veronique*: each time she swings back and forth she narrowly misses a man who is totally oblivious to her trajectory. The opening moments of *Jumpers* show George's Secretary doing a striptease on a swing and each time she comes into view she, too just avoids a hairbreadth collison with Crouch, the porter, who is perambulating with a drink's tray. Later, McFee's corpse is hooked to Dotty's bedroom-cupboard door and each time George closes the main bedroom door the cupboard door swings perilously open: this takes one back to the old Dhery sketch (later adopted by the Crazy gang) of a group of monastic bell-ringers who each time they pulled the extreme left bell would send the man holding the one on the extreme right shooting skywards.

There are other influences at work: Jonathan Miller's loping, rangy, limb-contorting parody of A.J. Ayer in *Beyond The Fringe*; the TV series *The Avengers*, (which, like *Jumpers*, starred Diana Rigg), which almost always began with an antic, pre-credit sequence murder which was then rationally explored; Joe Orton's *Loot*, which patented the idea of the bone-headed, myopic police inspector strangely oblivious to the evidence in front of him, though it must be admitted Orton's Inspector was far more lethally corrupt than Stoppard's; and the strange incongruities afforded by 1960s TV chat-shows where – as on one memorable occasion during *The Eamonn Andrews Show*

A.J.P. Taylor was placed next to Eartha Kitt – scholars might rub shoulders with songstresses.

I cite these examples not to prove that Stoppard is derivative but to establish that *Jumpers* is a remarkable theatrical concoction in which songs, striptease, whodunnit, gymnastics, good and bad puns are all put to the service of a play about belief and about the terrors of living in a pragmatic, expedient universe in which the old moral convictions are losing their restraining force. It is, I believe, a play about a disintegrating, modern world. Stoppard doesn't so much spell this out literally as flesh it out through a series of eye-popping images. Shaw, of course, before him, took popular theatrical forms such as drawing-room comedy and melodrama and hoodwinked the customers by injecting into them moral debate. But Shaw always stayed (with the arguable exception of *Misalliance* and *Too True To Be Good*) within accepted conventions; whereas Stoppard puts together what looks a bit like a ragbag revue and then underpins it with a debate about the nature of the universe we currently inhabit. There is a kind of logic under the anarchy.

Francis King, a very logical critic, pinned down the three main strands in the play when reviewing the 1985 production: 'Firstly, Moore and, to a lesser degree, his philosophical opponent and cuckold, the atheist Vice Chancellor of the University, hold forth at witty length about their views. Secondly, there is the murder of one of the 'jumpers' or acrobats, the materialistic Professor of Logic, with the consequent attempt of a spoof detective to find the culprit. Thirdly, there is the existential despair of Moore's actress wife Dorothy at the deromanticisation of the moon now that astronauts have landed on it.'

That is a beautifully clear summation of the play – what it misses out is the way Stoppard interweaves all three plot-strands to produce a deliberately fractured narrative corresponding to the crumbling values of the world he describes; a narrative which, nevertheless, has its own built-in logic. As Diana Rigg astutely observed in 1972: 'Everything in this play is perfectly logical. Everything ties in but it doesn't tie in in the sequence that we, as theatre-people, or you, as theatre-goers, are used to. More often than not the clue to the person's dilemma comes 35 minutes *before* the fact which is a complete inversion of how it's normally done.'

Absolutely; and, to prove the point, it is worth looking at the apparently random sequence of events in the first ten minutes of the play before George begins his lecture because out of them the play's themes evolve. We see the much-loved star of the musical-stage, Dorothy Moore, drying on any song lyric that contains the word 'moon': at first, it looks as if she is just a glamorous showbiz wreck; we realise later that she is both driven to despair by the implications of the moon-landings and is herself craving an understanding of her plight which she doesn't get from George. We then see a display of jumping, tumbling, somersaulting from the eight 'Incredible-Radical-Liberal-Jumpers'. In purely theatrical terms this is astonishing since we don't expect a play to begin with feats of physical daring. The logic of this, again, becomes clear later when we learn from George that the jumpers are 'logical positivists mainly, with a linguistic analyst or two, a couple of Benthamite utilitarians, lapsed Kantians and empiricists generally and, of course, behaviourists.' In other words, their acrobatics represent the ingenious but rather fanciful and sterile contortions demanded by their various systems. They are also, be it noted, Radical-Liberals which represents – as far as one can judge on the evidence available – a steely, utilitarian, technocratic party with strong anti-democratic tendencies, a dislike of the irrational and a determination to make an agnostic Archbishop of Canterbury. Their pyramid crumbles when one of their number is shot: as we learn later, this is the logician McFee whose philosophical stance is that murder is prohibited more by social convention than by moral imperative though he has been showing recidivist tendencies in the light of the anarchy unleashed by pragmatism. We then move into Dotty's bedroom which both contains a dead body and a TV set projecting the most extraordinary images: on the one hand, the triumphal procession of the Rad-Libs and, on the other, astronauts scrapping on the moon with Captain Scott knocking his subordinate Oates to the ground and pulling up the ladder to his vehicle with the words 'I am going up now. I may be gone for some time.' It hardly needs remarking that this is an inversion of the famous heroic myth of Captain Scott of the Antarctic meeting his end with stiff upper-lip courage and describing in his journal Lawrence Oates walking to his death as 'the act of a brave man and an English gentleman.' We then hear Dotty in her bedroom uttering panic-stricken cries of 'Help. Murder' (literally true of course) which George first ignores, next crosses to the bedroom door to cope with, and then, shuts out in order to get on with his lecture: 'To begin at the beginning: is God?'

As in *Lord Malquist and Mr Moon* and *After Magritte*, Stoppard bombards us with data and sensations and then only makes their pattern and meaning clear as the play progresses. In *Jumpers* the first ten minutes clearly state the play's theme: disintegration. This is a world in which singers can't sing, acrobats get shot, moon men tussle in a *sauve qui peut* situation. Stoppard is clearly telling us the world is out of joint. The question is: what made it that way?

The answer comes as the play progresses: that a world that denies the metaphysical absolutes of good and evil, that sunders any tolerance of the irrational, that subverts moral sanctions and that recklessly explores space without thought to the consequences is one that will fall into chaos. Time and again, Stoppard's early plays have dwelt on the fragility of society: now he shows society falling apart. Stoppard, himself always thought of as a relativist in political and moral matters, in *Jumpers* declares his hand: the play is as much a warning as Ulysses's speech on degree in *Troilus and Cressida*.

If this is so, it is clear that George's putative lecture is not a send-up of academic tics and convoluted thought: it is actually central to the matter in hand. My only cavil about Michael Hordern's performance in the original production and the 1976 revival is that it tended to become a collection of funny comic mannerisms as he scratched and fussed his way towards understanding: Paul Eddington in the 1985 production was better because you felt he cared deeply about the content of his speech and, at the same time, was deeply distraught at the prospect of his wife's infidelity. George is trying to find logical support for his belief in two Gods: one to create the world and another to sustain his moral values. He cannot definitively find that support but you have to follow the stages of his argument and understand that he is a man of passion, as evidenced when Dotty quotes Archie's view that the church is a monument to irrationality:

GEORGE: 'The National Gallery is a monument to irrationality. Every concert hall is a monument to irrationality – and so is a nicely kept garden, or a lover's favour, or a home for stray dogs. You stupid woman, if rationality were the criterion for things being allowed to exist, the world would be one gigantic field of soya beans.

(*He picks up his tortoise and balances it lovingly on the palm of his hand, at the level of his mouth.*)

(*Apologetically.*) Wouldn't it, Pat?

The irrational, the emotional, the whimsical ... these are the stamp of humanity which makes reason a civilising force. In a wholly rational society, the moralist will be a variety of crank, haranguing the bus queue with the demented certitude of one blessed with privileged information – "Good and evil are metaphysical absolutes'. What did I come in for?'

That is one of those cherishable moments in Stoppard when an authentic feeling breaks through the patina of jocularity and argument.

What is good about *Jumpers* is that everything feeds into the central argument. Stoppard is able to interweave the philosophical enquiry, the murder investigation and Dotty's breakdown. Thus, when Inspector Bones arrives to investigate the murder that has taken place, George gives him a coherent rundown of his opponent McFee's belief that telling truth and not killing people are social and psychological conventions, 'in much the same way as we have evolved the rules of tennis without which Wimbledon Fortnight would be a complete shambles.' He explains that *philosophically* McFee would not argue that killing people is actually wrong: the double-irony is, of course, that George is explaining all this when there is a corpse in his wife's bedroom and that McFee has been hoist with his own petard. A philosophical viewpoint is being put across at the same time as the plot is itself being advanced.

Stoppard's play is very much concerned to demonstrate the practical consequences of philosophical beliefs and throughout the play death is very much the litmus-test. The play, as we have noted, starts with two murders: those of McFee and Oates. And if you take the logician's view that killing is impractical rather than morally wrong, then there is nothing to stop you doing what

Archie and the choreographed Jumpers do, which is to throw a corpse into a plastic bag – produced as in a conjuring trick from Archie's pocket – and go and dump it in Hyde Park. But equally George's humanity is established through his (wholly irrational) devotion to his tortoise, Pat, and his hare, Thumper. The two animals are not randomly selected since George uses them to demonstrate Zeno's notion of infinite series, 'which showed in every way but experience that an arrow could never reach its target and that a tortoise given a head start in a race with, say, a hare could never be overtaken.' In proving the nonsensical nature of the first theory George accidentally kills both animals. Early on in the play he raises his bow to prove that an arrow does reach its target, lays it aside and only releases the arrow when the attention-seeking Dotty cries 'Fire.' The arrow goes over the top of the wardrobe and is forgotten. Until, that is, the very end of the play when George sees blood on his Secretary's coat, realises that it has come from the top of the wardrobe and discovers Thumper impaled on a mis-fired arrow. Appalled at his discovery, he steps backward and crunches underfoot the momentarily-forgotten Pat. George's grief at two dead animals is the precise antithesis of Archie's coolness at a dead logician; and the act ends with George echoing Dotty's cry of 'Help. Murder' and sobbing profusely. This confirms the play's logical structure and Stoppard's deliberate opposition of attitudes to death.

Stoppard is writing about the dangers of living in a moral limbo and exhibiting its practical consequences. His concern itself is not new. It dates back, at least, to *Lord Malquist and Mr Moon* where the impotent hero explains his bomb-throwing proclivities by saying 'it's something to do with no one being *good* any more, but that's part of the other thing, of things all getting out of control, too big.' The suicide-prone Fraser in *Albert's Bridge* also warned 'Civilisation is in decline and the white rhino is being wiped out for the racket in bogus aphrodisiacs.' In the past, Stoppard characters have taken refuge from disorder, chaos, the multiplicity of things, the collapse of decency by entering hospitals, writing books, painting bridges or attempting to throw themselves off them; in *Jumpers* there is some attempt, however vain, to combat moral inertia and uncertainty. George argues the case for a God of goodness: Dotty issues frantic cries for help. Even the dead

McFee has woken up belatedly to the consequences of his materialist philosophy as the porter Crouch explains:

> 'It was the astronauts fighting on the Moon that finally turned him, sir. Henry, he said to me, Henry, I am giving philosophical respectability to a new pragmatism in public life, of which there have been many disturbing examples both here and on the moon. Duncan, I said, Duncan, don't let it get you down, have another can of beer. But he kept harking back to the first Captain Oates, out there in the Antarctic wastes, sacrificing his life to give his companions a slim chance of survival . . . Henry, he said, what made him do it? – out of the tent and into the jaws of the blizzard. If altruism is a possibility, he said, my argument is up a gum tree . . . Duncan, I said, Duncan, don't you worry your head about all that. That astronaut yobbo is good for twenty years hard. Yes, he said, yes *maybe* but when he comes out he's going to find he was only twenty years ahead of his time. I have seen the future, Henry, he said; and it's yellow.'

That speech, even more than Dotty's attack on the consequences of the moon-landings, is the keynote of the play.

Jumpers argues the case for moral sanctions with surface razzle-dazzle and verbal wit but is it actually a good play? Any work that takes on board so many complex ideas while keeping us entertained for two-and-a-half hours has to have a lot going for it. Seeing the play in various productions, however, induces reservations. The first concerns Stoppard's shadowy definition of the Radical-Liberal Party who, as far as we can make out, stand for rationalisation of the Church, suppression of press-freedom, the imprisonment of property speculators and Masters of Foxhounds. What Stoppard has done is to create a fictive, bogey-party that sounds like a parody of the Loony Left but that corresponds to nothing in the world of political reality. This is right-wing scaremongering that was pretty far-fetched even in 1972 and that looks even more dated in the Britain of the 1980s: indeed, by a wonderful stroke of historical irony, the church is now under threat not from the political Left but from the Right who bitterly resent its moral stand against poverty, deprivation and unemployment. Far from being the Tory Party at prayer, the Church of England is now regarded by many on the Right as a dangerously subversive organisation as packed with pinkos and Lefties as their fantasy-version of the BBC.

Even more crucial to our assessment of *Jumpers* is the absurdity of Dotty's thesis that the moon-landings will lead to moral mayhem 'because the truths that have been taken on trust, they've never had edges before'. Even when *Jumpers* was premièred it was a pretty way-out notion. In the play Dotty asks George 'Do you think it is . . . *significant* that it's impossible to imagine anyone building a church on the moon?'; but *Time* revealed in November 1971 that one of astronaut Buzz Aldrin's first actions on the moon was to practise a Communion ceremony with bread and wine. 'I poured the wine into the chalice which our church had given me,' said Aldrin. 'In the one-sixth gravity of the moon, the wine curled slowly and gracefully up the side of the cup. It was interesting to think that the very first liquid ever poured on the moon and the first food eaten there were Communion elements.' What with Communion on the one hand and the practising of golf-shots on the other, the moon-landings suggest the transportation of earthly values to another place. In discussing *Another Moon Called Earth* I suggested that the American moon-landings had hardly been the cause of a moral apocalypse. If Western civilization is in a state of Spenglerian decline, it has – I venture – less to do with space exploration than with the failure of governments to tackle the problems of crime, poverty and unemployment and with the commercialisation of a culture that offers people limitless supplies of junk-television, junk-food, junk-music. In a special issue devoted to listing the 'Best of America', *Time* (again) in June, 1986 cited pop-culture and, in particular, the elevation of the movie-hero, Rambo, to mythic status: 'Today America's righteous pop thug is huge, ubiquitous, swaggering from one medium to the next and the next: he is a movie warrior, he is a TV cartoon character, he is a plastic doll, he is a music-video creature and now, in candy-racks all over America, he is chewing-gum.' When a 'thug' becomes an icon, then you can talk about a declining civilisation; but I don't believe you can pin that on Aldrin and Armstrong or the rise of logical positivism.

Stoppard in 1972 spotted the malaise at the heart of our civilisation; but I find his diagnosis hard to accept. The other problem with *Jumpers* is whether the characters and story are strong enough to bear the intellectual weight they have to carry? Do we care enough about George and Dotty as *people* to worry about the moral dilemmas they articulate and represent? The answer, in theatrical terms, is Yes and No. George does exist fully as a character capable both of passion and pathos. Michael Hordern in the original production – looking, said J.C. Trewin, 'like a cross between a tired bloodhound, a worried owl and the late Sir Alan Herbert' – was a very funny composite of academic mannerisms. But Tom Courtenay, in the 1984 Royal Exchange production, discovered in the role a quality of spiritual passion. When he came to the defence of irrational concepts like art and religion, his pouchy features took on a flush of angry excitement; and when, in the final dream-sequence, he attacked the moral relativists who claim to 'know' that life is better than death while at the same time arguing that knowledge is only a possibility in matters that can be demonstrated to be true or false, his voice hit the crucial verb in a scream of frustration. And when Paul Eddington played George at the Aldwych in 1985 he both steered us through the labyrinthine complexity of Moore's arguments and brought out the man's sheer gut-wrenching agony from his suspicions of his wife's adultery.

The problem is Dotty whom I have seen played any number of ways. Diana Rigg oozed glamour, intelligence and wit. Julie Covington in the 1976 National Theatre revival had a fragile pathos but less of the showbiz-star side of Dotty. Julie Walters in the 1984 Manchester production presented us with a raging head-case but not someone whom you could imagine sitting astride crescent-moons. Felicity Kendal in 1985 was a satiny, seductive tease but her lunar fixation did not carry too much weight. The trouble is Dotty is an idea more than a real person: a broken-down singer, a teasing sexpot, a woman actively concerned at moral decline, a possible murderess. She simply doesn't add up. At one point in the play, she is a spokesperson for Archie's philosophy that good and bad, better and worse are not the real properties of things but just an expression of our feelings about them: at another, she is concerned precisely because our saving moral absolutes look like, 'the local customs of another place'. The attitudes are irreconcileable; and one concludes that, at this stage of his career, Stoppard has still to write a totally convincing female character.

A critical balance-sheet on *Jumpers*, would show Stoppard definitely in the black. The play is audacious, funny, inventive. It expresses a point of view: that a society that dismisses God as a logical impossibility, and moral absolutes as unprovable, is more likely to fracture and splinter than one that doesn't. It also presents us with an image of disintegration that is held together by a hidden structural logic: extract any particular sequence or line from the play and it would implode on the missing part rather like the pyramid of acrobats. It is not the only form of drama but it is not quite like anything else in the modern repertoire. It also tends to prove the truth of what Francis Bacon said in his Essays: 'A little philosophy inclineth man's mind to atheism but depth in philosophy bringeth men's minds about to religion.'

Artist Descending a Staircase

Stoppard might have had some sympathy with that Francis Bacon. On the evidence of his radio play *Artist Descending a Staircase* (first broadcast on Radio 3 on November 14, 1972) I doubt whether he cares much for the other Francis Bacon: the painter of twisted, tortured, agonised, corkscrewed human figures. For this play is radical in form but conservative in content: a diabolically clever work that, at the same time, savagely lampoons modern art. In many ways, it is a dry run for a later play *Travesties* in that it deals with the fallibility of memory, the subjectivity of perception, the proper function of the artist, the self-indulgence of modernism. The odd thing about Stoppard is that he scorns experiment in the visual arts while himself being a persistent mould-breaker when it comes to theatre and radio.

I can, for instance, think of no radio play in history constructed quite like this one. Its eleven scenes are arranged in a very precise symmetrical shape. Scenes one and eleven are set in the here and now; scenes two and ten a couple of hours ago; three and nine last week; four and eight in 1922; five and seven in 1920 and the pivotal scene six in 1914. So, as Stoppard says, the temporal sequence is ABCDEFEDCBA. The drama carries us back in time and then slowly forwards. It is like a rubber-ball attached to a hand by a piece of elastic hurled in one direction and then returning whence it came. It is highly ingenious even if there is an element of 'My God, isn't that clever' about the listener's reaction.

As so often in his plays, Stoppard uses a whodunnit as a framework for a discussion of serious matters: I am reminded of the Californian goldminers who, on hearing from Oscar Wilde that Andrea del Sarto was dead, instinctively enquired 'Who shot him?' In the opening scene we hear Beauchamp, an elderly experimenter in 'tonal art', and Martello, an even more senile sculptor, (both men named after towers, incidentally) playing back a tape recording the death of their old live-in companion, the painter Donner: on the tape we hear Donner crying out 'Ah, there you are', falling through a balustrade and hitting the ground with a sickening thud. Who killed him? Beauchamp thinks Martello did it: Martello suspects Beauchamp. Either man might have had a motive. Donner, after enjoying his years in 'that child's garden of easy victories known as the avant-garde' has now returned to 'traditional values .. where the whole history of art continues to lie.' He dismisses the work of his two old friends as rubbish: Beauchamp creates tapes full of bubbles, squeaks, gurgles and crackles, Martello has been making a metaphorical sculpture – using ripe corn for the hair, artificial pearls for the teeth, fruit for the breasts and real feathers for the swan-like neck – out of a girl called Sophie whom Donner once unrequitedly loved.

We then flash back 50 years to discover that Sophie was a blind girl who threaded her way through the lives of all three artists. She met them at the time of their first exhibition, 'Frontiers in Art' which jokingly consisted of paintings of barbed-wire fences and signboards saying 'You are now entering Patagonia'. Martello was the one who first discovered Sophie; Beauchamp was the one she fell in love with, dimly peering at him posed against his picture of a black border-fence in the snow; Donner was the one who loved her hopelessly. Receding further back in time we find these three figures (a mixture of Jerome K. Jerome's boating trio and Murger's characters in *Scènes de la vie de Bohème*) careering through Europe in 1914 myopically misunderstanding the obvious signs of impending war. The play then moves gradually forward in time revealing Sophie's tragic defenestration in 1922, her growth as a symbol of beauty in all the men's memories and the fact that she may, in truth, have loved Donner all along since he once posed against a picture of thick white posts against a black background, confusingly similar to Beauchamp's. Finally – back in the here and now – we realise that Donner was not murdered but fell to his death in the act of swatting a fly.

This is pure radio in that the resolution of the mystery depends

Rosencrantz and Guildenstern Are Dead (Young Vic, 1974)

The Real Inspector Hound (National Theatre, Olivier, 1985)

Travesties (Aldwych, 1974)

Jumpers (National Theatre, Old Vic, 1974)

Dirty Linen (Almost Free, 1976)

Night and Day (Aldwych, 1974)

Every Good Boy Deserves Favour (Mermaid, 1978)

Cahoot's Macbeth (Collegiate Theatre, 1979)

On the Razzle (National Theatre, Lyttelton, 1981)

Undiscovered Country (National Theatre, Olivier, 1979)

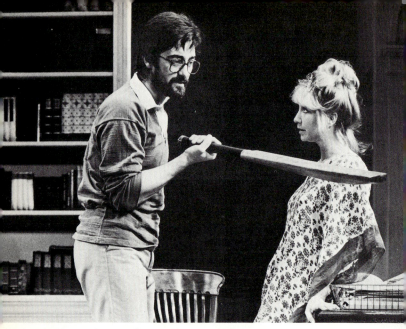

The Real Thing (Strand Theatre, 1982)

Dalliance (National Theatre, Lyttelton, 1986)

upon the elucidation of a sound-effect. Throughout, Stoppard plays tricks with our aural sensations: the scene 'last week' ends with Donner hymning 'a phrase of music . . . a river flowing beneath ancient bridges . . . the scent of summer time' with, underneath, cliché Paris music and an accordion. The next scene, in 1922, starts with Sophie – to the same accompaniment – saying 'I must say I won't be entirely sorry to leave Lambeth – the river smells like a dead cat and the accordionist downstairs is driving me insane.' You couldn't achieve a joke like that in any other medium.

That plays a trick upon the listener. But it is also at the heart of the play which is about the subjectivity of perception. A misheard tape-recording leads to accusations of murder and mutual recrimination. Sophie has ruined her life and that of two other people by falling for a man in front of a picture of black posts against a white background when it was really a man in front of white posts against a black background. The three heroes traverse Europe in 1914 totally misreading the preparations for war and seeing convoys of lorries and squadrons of cavalry as no more than a petty squabble over frontiers. Like Henry Carr in *Travesties* they fail to perceive history while it is happening. Stoppard's larger point is that there is almost no such animal as objective truth and we see almost everything through the often-clouded prism of our prejudices and preconceptions.

That applies to art as much as to life; and what Stoppard is also doing in this radical-conservative play is opening up an enquiry into the function of art and the role of the artist. Donner is the loony experimenter turned traditional painter; Beauchamp is the zany aural pioneer; Martello is the creator of scarecrow-like sculptures. But although the debate is eminently worthwhile and Stoppard says many pregnant, discussable things, he short-circuits the argument by deliberately choosing far-out examples of modern art: this is pile-of-bricks-in-the-Tate time. Donner says at one point, 'Skill without imagination is craftsmanship and gives us many useful objects such as wickerwork picnic baskets. Imagination without skill gives us modern art.' I swallowed hard when I first heard that but put it down as the point of view of the character. When Stoppard was confronted by that quote by Mel Gussow in a *New York Times* interview in 1984 he said unequivocally, 'I believe that.'

It would be interesting to know where Stoppard draws the line in modern art. Imagination without skill in the work of Picasso, Munch, Magritte, Chagall, Miro, de Chirico, Vlaminck, Klee, Nash, Beckmann, Bacon, Moore, Hockney, Rouault, Kokoschka, Pollock, de Kooning, Klein, Mondrian or Modigliani? Anyone can point to examples of pseudery and pretension in modern art but to rubbish a whole movement smacks of pop-press philistinism. Not everyone is making sculpture out of tin-tacks or riding motor-bikes over their canvasses; and, if they are, what of it? How a work is achieved matters less than the impression it makes. I recall David Sylvester saying on television that a painting or sculpture is vindicated when it gives the spectator a pleasing visual impression. Art is not something that can be restricted, codified or narrowed down to precise definitions. As Conrad Fiedler wrote in 1887 art is 'an ever-living question asked of the visible world by the visual sense.' And, in Herbert Read's gloss on that quote, 'the artist is simply the man who has the ability and the desire to transform his visual perception into material form.'

I see Stoppard's point: that craft has to be allied to imagination. But here he doesn't so much set up a debate as load the dice by implying that modern art is a lot of over-indulged people turning out tapes full of jumbled sound, making sculpture from *objets trouvés* or hewing shapes out of sugar. 'It will give cubism a new lease of life' says Martello though personally I would have said it was more Tate than Lyle. In seeking to emphasise that art is nothing without skill Stoppard comes up with his own elaborate definition: 'An artist is someone who is gifted in some way which enables him to do something more or less well which can only be done badly or not at all by someone who is not thus gifted.' It was Kenneth Tynan who pointed out that could apply equally well to a jockey: he might have added a steeplejack, a fighter pilot, an orthodontist, a masseuse or myriad other professions that call upon some special gift.

We are dealing with a play, not a discussion-paper; but a play must also be judged by its truthfulness and when a dramatist talks nonsense one should say so. Stoppard is fully entitled to dismiss large chunks of modern art as a talentless fraud; but when he chooses as an example Martello's idea of creating a wooden man with a real leg to be called 'The Cripple' I tend to think he is weakening a general case by the use of an extreme example. In *Travesties* he gives house-room to several different theories about art and sets up a genuine tension between them. In this play he sets Donner up against a couple of amiable avant-garde way-outers and allows him to score easy points.

This is not to say that *Artist Descending a Staircase* is, by any means, negligible. It offers interesting ideas about the fallibility of perception. It has some genuinely funny lines. It anticipates a crucial Stoppard theme which is 'that small sense of shame with which every artist lives.' But, above all, it is, in its own way, a rather avant-garde piece of radio making unusual demands upon the listener through being constructed, as Paul Ferris noted, like a poem whose first and last lines rhyme until the rhymes meet in the middle. Stoppard is reactionary in his arguments but adventurous in his technique; which makes it slightly odd that he should be so scathing about other artists who seek to push the frontiers of the possible outwards.

Travesties

Plays are not static objects: they change their meaning, their quality, their importance with time and successive revivals. This is certainly true of *Travesties* which underwent something of a sea-change between my first experience of it at the Aldwych on June 10, 1974 and my most recent encounter with it at Oxford Playhouse in January, 1986. The text remains virtually the same; the play still exerts considerable fascination, but when I first saw it I was mesmerised by John Wood's performance (in a role tailored especially to his abundant ironic energy) and by Stoppard's ability to cram in so many different styles and themes. Here was a play that combined Wildean parody, political lecture, spoof reminiscence, song-and-dance. Here was a play that dealt with the fallibility of memory, the role of the artist, the logical flaw in Marxist revolution, the relativity of language, the aesthetic conservatism of political revolutionaries, the absurdity of history when seen from the sidelines. When I saw the play again twelve years later – in one of its few major revivals – it seemed much less a star-vehicle and much more a kaleidoscopic debate on the question of whether the artist can ever be the architect of social, or indeed, literary change. It picks up many of the ideas aired in *Artist Descending a Staircase*. But it offers them greater discussion-time; and I propose to pursue Stoppard's debate on the artist's function.

The play starts, of course, from the historical fact that Lenin, Joyce and the Dadaist Tristan Tzara were all living in Zurich during the Great War. It also takes as its hero, Henry Carr, someone who was indisputably real although Stoppard has woven a fictive character around him. The facts are that James Joyce became business manager of The English Players who put on a production of *The Importance of Being Earnest* on April 29, 1918 at the Theater Zur Kaufleuten in Zurich. The role of Algernon Moncrieff was undertaken by a minor consular official, Henry Carr, who enjoyed a great success but subsequently was involved in litigation with Joyce. Carr claimed reimbursement for the cost of some trousers he had purchased for the role or, alternatively, a share of the profits: Joyce counter-claimed for the price of five tickets sold by Carr and also sued him for slander. Joyce won on the money but lost on the slander; and reserved his revenge for *Ulysses* where he mentions a Private Carr who refers with insubordinate disrespect to his Sergeant-Major, Bennett – the name of the Consul-General in Zurich at the time.

That much is well-known. What is significant is Stoppard's delight – as in *Rosencrantz and Guildenstern* – in glimpsing major events from the sidelong perspective of someone only marginally involved with them. There is not a shred of evidence that Carr ever met either Lenin or Tzara; but in later life he likes to think he might have done and that – with slightly more prompt action on his part – he might have forestalled the Russian Revolution. Rather like Woody Allen in *Zelig* caught waving frantically from behind Hitler's back at a Nuremburg Rally, Stoppard likes to place his figures against the backcloth of major events: the machinations of Elsinore, Churchill's funeral, a *coup d'état* by the Radical-Liberals, Zurich in ferment. It is as if Stoppard is reminding us that historical events always look slightly preposterous when seen from the margins.

Stoppard also picked up what many critics failed to notice which is the structural similarity between *Travesties* and his previous full-length play. *Jumpers* and *Travesties*,' he told Ronald Hayman in 1975, 'are very similar plays. No-one's said that but they're so similar that were I to do it a third time it would be a bore. You start with a prologue which is slightly strange. Then you have an interminable monologue which is rather funny. Then you have scenes. Then you end up with another monologue. And you have unexpected bits of music and dance, and at the same time people are playing ping-pong with various intellectual arguments.' A very fair summary of the way *Travesties* works.

But what fascinates me is Stoppard's obsessive concern with art and artists. The theme first surfaces in the jumbled, erratic recollections of Henry Carr whose memory of James Joyce starts with a pious tribute to his genius and proceeds to waspish irritation: 'In short, a complex personality, an enigma, a contradictory spokesman for the truth, an obsessive litigant and yet an essentially private man who wished his total indifference to public notice to be universally recognised.' One is reminded, as quite often, of Alan Bennett's historical revue, *Forty Years On*, where great events are also seen through the faulty prism of memory and where it is said of Lawrence of Arabia that 'Clad in the magnificent white silk robes of an Arab prince, with in his belt the short, curved, gold sword of the Ashraf descendants of the Prophet, he hopes to pass unnoticed through London.' Carr's memories of the great have a similarly puncturing effect and Alan Bennett-type jokes pop their heads above the parapet: Dada was, topographically speaking, the high point of Western culture because Tzara wrote his name in the snow with a walking stick and said 'There. I think I'll call it The Alps.'

The first, major engagement with the subject of art comes when Tristan Tzara visits Henry Carr; and what is instantly striking is how Stoppard takes ideas adumbrated in the debate between Donner and Beauchamp in *Artist Descending a Staircase* and expands them into a five-minute, head-on collision in which both participants are equally eloquent. The question of where Stoppard's own sympathies lie is less important than the fact that each man caps the other's arguments and that Stoppard enjoys writing Tzara just as much as he does Carr.

Carr's opening gambit is that all art involves a degree of benevolent neutrality and non-engagement in the great issues. Tzara rallies by expanding the definition of art to 'Nowadays an artist is someone who makes art mean the things he does.' To which Carr's retort is that this is simply a perversion of language and that one might just as well be able to claim to fly even though one has no capacity for propelling oneself about while suspended in the air: you cannot make Art mean whatever you wish it to mean. 'Why not?' asks Tzara. 'You do exactly the same with words like *patriotism*, *duty*, *love*, *freedom*, king and country, brave little Belgium, saucy little Serbia.' Carr comes back with the fact that wars are fought not for words but for civilised ideals and making the world safe for artists. Not at all, cries Tzara, 'war is capitalism with the gloves off' and is fought for oil wells and coaling-stations. Heatedly, Carr retorts with the fact that war cannot be encapsulated in empty phrases and that he and his like went to war to protect the boring Belgians and incompetent Frogs from German militarism. Stormingly, Tzara comes back with the fact that the real origins of the First World War lay in the Archduke Franz-Ferdinand's marriage in 1900 and his determination to have his wife riding beside him on his wedding anniversary on June 28, 1914 when he inspected the Austro-Hungarian army in Bosnia.

This is good writing: Stoppard doing what he is always claimed to do by giving us mutually contradictory points of view with uninflected fairness. One of the keys to real drama is the presentation of equally balanced arguments: Shaw was a master of it and used the technique most brilliantly in *Saint Joan* where Cauchon's arguments as to why Joan cannot be the private interceptor between the Church and God are matched by Joan's passionate defence of nonconformist individualism. Stoppard here also starts with a private collision on the function of art and then extends it, almost imperceptibly, to take on board the subjectivity of language and the origins of war. The point is neither Carr nor Tzara is exclusively right or wrong. Carr has a point that words have to be used with precision: Tzara has a point that certain concepts are prone to subjective coloration. Carr has a point that people enlist because of an impulsive sense of duty: Tzara has a point that wars are caused by some connecting chain of events. Carr may be right that art is, in the end, irrelevant to history: Tzara may also be right that the meaning of the word 'art' is now all-embracing. Stoppard, like a good dramatist, hurls the ideas at us and leaves us to pick our way through them.

As the discourse between Carr and Tzara continues, I must confess my own sympathies lie less and less with Carr's notion of the artist as some kind of hothouse specimen: neutral, disengaged and afflicted with exaggerated notions of self-importance. 'Revolution in art,' says Carr, 'is in no way connected with *class* revolution. Artists are members of a privileged class. Art is absurdly overrated by artists, which is understandable, but what is strange is that it is absurdly overrated by everyone else.' What Carr's vision (maybe Stoppard's too) overlooks is the extent to which our idea of ourselves and our society is actually shaped and formed by art and the way our own experiences of the world are reflected back by art. Sometimes we forget these simple truths. It was fascinating to find Anthony Burgess (in a newspaper review, ironically enough, of a new edition of *Ulysses*) writing, 'The other night I watched *King Lear* on Italian television and saw a greatness I could not be aware of when I was a Manchester schoolboy and ignorant of what cruelties lay in store for the world.'

One could multiply examples of the two-way process of art: both shaping our experience of the world and defining it. A man who has read or seen *Hamlet* is more likely to understand the dilemma of the spirit paralysed by inaction and of the discrepancy between violent means and necessary ends, than one who hasn't. A man who has heard Beethoven's Ninth Symphony is more likely to comprehend human capacity for joy than someone who is ignorant or tone-deaf. A man who has looked at Impressionist paintings is more likely to see the way our perception of buildings, landscapes and people is affected by the play of light on surfaces than one who hasn't. Stoppard himself shows in this play that he sees there is more to the artist than Carr's vision of him as a privileged dilettante and Tristan Tzara's notion of him as the anti-artist, the destroyer of reason and causality. Through the character of James Joyce – initially seen as a comic caperer wearing discordant clothes and conversing in equally discordant limericks – he does offer an alternative notion of the artist as a magician put amongst men to gratify their urge for immortality:

'What now of the Trojan War if it has been passed over by the artist's touch? Dust. A forgotten expedition prompted by Greek merchants looking for new markets. A minor redistribution of broken pots. But it is we who stand enriched, by a tale of heroes, of a golden apple, a wooden horse, a face that launched a thousand ships – and, above

101

all, of Ulysses the wanderer, the most human, the most complete of all heroes – husband, father, son, lover, farmer, soldier, pacifist, politician, inventor and adventurer ... It is a theme so overwhelming that I am almost afraid to treat it. And yet I with my Dublin Odyssey will double that immortality, yes by God *there's* a corpse that will dance for some time yet and *leave the world precisely as it finds it.*'

That seems to me a potent argument; and Stoppard admits that temperamentally and intellectually he is very much on Joyce's side. Yet I find the italicised emphasis on those last few words very strange. How can *Ulysses* be said to have left the world as it found it? Is changing people's consciousness and extending the range of the novel not as much a way of affecting the world as passing a piece of legislation? Is not Joyce still remembered when the pettifogging puritans who attacked him are forgotten? As Cyril Connolly once pointed out, in America and in Paris a whole *Ulysses*-generation grew up. Even more pointedly, Connolly wrote of 'the enthusiasm which comes to everyone when they discover themselves through a book – a service which Joyce, Proust and Gide have rendered generally to almost all our thinking generation.' Joyce enlarged our vision; and that seems to me a legitimate way of changing the world.

Stoppard's rich play brings in yet another attitude to art, Lenin's – taken directly from remarks he made in 1905 at the time of the first revolution – which puts the case for what Stalin would later call the artist as 'social engineer'. Unsurprisingly, this attacks the notion of the artist as bourgeois individual and substitutes the notion of him as someone who is an instrument and voice for the party. 'Literature,' trumpets Lenin, 'must become a part of the common cause of the proletariat, a cog in the Social Democratic mechanism.' Few people, other than Marxist hardliners, would endorse that particular line of thinking. And when Lenin says, 'Socialist literature and art will be free because the idea of socialism and sympathy with the working people, instead of greed and careerism, will bring ever new forces to its ranks' one is tempted to think of all the artists persecuted by totalitarianism. And yet the reality is more complex than a simple abhorrence of the Leninist line admits. I have seen, with my own eyes, modern Soviet or East European plays and films that deal satirically with social and political problems and that present human relationships more compassionately than many of our artefacts in the West: it is a recognised fact that circumscription and censorship breeds its own resistance and that art will always find ways of evading the most restrictive laws. Before we laugh Lenin off the stage, we have to ask ourselves whether, for instance, the insane preoccupation with destructiveness and cruelty in modern American cinema is preferable to the lyricism and poignancy often found in party-controlled Soviet films.

Stoppard offers us multiple perspectives in *Travesties*. If he comes to any conclusion, it is that political and artistic revolutions are entirely different entitites. The Dadaists unavailingly tried to knock the supports from under the foundations of bourgeois society: Lenin, the political revolutionary, was an artistic reactionary who deliberately cut himself off from music because 'it affects my nerves, makes me want to say nice stupid things and pat the heads of those people who while living in this vile hell can create such beauty.' The dominant impression left by the play is that the artist is a privileged member of society; but however magnificent his achievement (as in the case of Joyce) it leaves the actual world just as it found it.

What Stoppard doesn't acknowledge is the power of art to unsettle and unnerve or to alter our vision of reality. Hans Arp put it dramatically in *The Naval Bottle*, 'The bourgeois regarded the Dadaist as a dissolute monster, a revolutionary villain, a barbarous Asiatic, plotting against his bells, his safe-deposits, his honours list. The Dadaist thought up tricks to rob the bourgeois of his sleep ... The Dadaist gave the bourgeois a sense of confusion and distant, yet mighty rumbling, so that his bells began to buzz, his safes frowned, and his honours list broke out in spots.'

Even allowing for a certain amount of vainglorious breast-beating on Arp's part, it is true that the Modernist movement in all the arts had a ripple effect: Futurism, Vorticism, Expressionism, Dada and Surrealism in the visual arts, atonalism in music, *vers libre* in poetry, fragmentation and stream of consciousness in the novel affected our way of seeing the world. A play like *Travesties*, fragmented and kaleidoscopic, would not have been conceivable without that movement. The impact of Modernism also spread way beyond the *aficionados* of the art world. The Armory Show in 1913 gave America its first taste of advanced

European art and a work like Marcel Duchamp's *Artist Descending a Staircase* caused outrage and uproar that spread far beyond the gallery-world. In Britain in the 1930s the intellectuals who joined the international Communist movement also often allied themselves with the artistic avant-garde. As Raymond Williams noted when reviewing Andrew Sinclair's book, *The Red and The Blue*: 'It was firmly believed, especially by the Surrealists, that to challenge, overthrow and replace bourgeois art-forms was to reveal a dynamic and finally revolutionary truth. The cross-over between Leninist notions of the vanguard and artistic versions of the avant-garde was, for Blunt and others, fertile ground for both affiliation and confusion in the relevant period.'

Stoppard generously gives us many different points of view in *Travesties*. The play is, amongst other things, an attack on socialist theories of art and one that plays slightly unfair in roping Oscar Wilde in on the side of the politically uncommitted. Henry Carr says to Cecily of Wilde that 'He may have been a little overdressed but he made up for it by being immensely uncommitted.' This is hardly the Oscar Wilde who wrote in *The Soul of Man Under Socialism*: 'Socialism, Communism or whatever one chooses to call it, by converting private property into public wealth and substituting co-operation for competition will restore society to its proper condition of a thoroughly healthy organism and ensure the natural well-being of each member of the community. It will in fact give Life its proper basis and its proper environment.'

I enjoy *Travesties* for its wit, its erudition, its interplay of argument, its highly theatrical combination of time-slips, potted history, striptease, song-and-dance. Tzara says an artist is someone who makes art mean the things he does: Stoppard is a dramatist who makes drama mean the things he does. Yet, seeing the play staged again at Oxford Playhouse in 1986, one became aware of how it goes into reverse gear in the second half with the arrival of Lenin and details of his progress to the Finland Station. There is no way that Lenin can be fitted into the overall Wildean framework. He is simply too massive a figure (one can say of him what the historian E.H. Carr said of Marx, 'he introduced into revolutionary theory and practice the order, method and authority which had hitherto been the prerogative of governments, and thereby laid the foundation of the disciplined revolutionary state') and his very presence fractures the play.

But one comes back to the fact that *Travesties* is a piece of theatre not an essay and, as such, it has provided moments of rare exhilaration. At the Aldwych in 1974-5, it gave John Wood as Henry Carr the role of a lifetime and I still recall Wood's diverse brilliance. Seizing on the fact that Joyce refused to stump up for Carr's expenditure on trousers, Mr Wood turned sartorial obsession into a sexual fetish, he almost masturbated at the thought of cream-flannel trousers and his voice quavered at the memory of what the Great War did to his heavy worsteds. The strength of his performance was that it combined rapid delivery and finicky articulation with a set of indelible images: the aged, reminiscent Carr chewing on endless cigarettes as if about to swallow them and the younger, debonair Carr, all spidery legs and angular elbows, moving through Zurich like a Beerbohm cartoon in perpetual motion. This was great acting. Seeing the play again at Oxford in 1986 I was impressed by Chris Hunter's Carr but even more by the way Richard Williams's production beefed up the other roles and turned the play into a phatasmagoria beginning with a Dadaist rendering of German numerals scored for typewriter, siren, whistle and cylinder. The play enshrined a debate in the form of a dream and offered a viable alternative to the hectic dazzle of Peter Wood's initial version. Whether *Travesties* will endure in the Stoppard canon is a matter of speculation: it lacks dramatic accumulation and that sense of pain and pathos that can be found under the glittering surface of *Jumpers*. You don't actually *feel* for anyone in *Travesties*. But the ultimate irony is that the play questions the social efficacy of the artist and the value of a committed political stance while Stoppard himself, in the years to come, was to turn into an *engagé* champion of human rights.

4

Summary Convictions

In the decade since his first play (*The Gamblers*) was performed at Bristol University and *A Walk on the Water* was done on radio, Stoppard had achieved an incredible amount: three hit-plays at the National and the RSC, a Prix Italia for *Albert's Bridge*, a substantial number of TV plays, a novel that deserved more readers than it got. He had also done translations of Mrozek's *Tango* and Lorca's *The House of Bernarda Alba* and made his first foray into direction with Garson Kanin's *Born Yesterday* at Greenwich Theatre. He gave interviews very readily, was photographed by Snowdon, had all the appurtenances of success without ever losing the sense of permanent insecurity that attends all good writers. But, as he himself was aware, he had in *Jumpers* and *Travesties* twice written similarly-structured extravaganzas. He needed to break the mould.

In 1975 he was represented by three very different works in television and cinema. He wrote, with Clive Exton, a TV play, *The Boundary*, about two lexicographers again attempting to structure the universe but finding their words, literally, blown in all directions. He also did a sober TV adaptation of Jerome K. Jerome's *Three Men in a Boat*. And that year saw the release of the film of *The Romantic Englishwoman*, which Stoppard scripted from a novel by Thomas Wiseman and which Joseph Losey directed. Saul Bellow, happening to be in London on his way back to America from Jerusalem, clearly saw it and chillingly recorded his impressions in *To Jerusalem and Back*:

'We decide on a Tom Stoppard movie; it is terrible. What we really wanted was to come in from the chill gull-gray street, eat chocolate in the dark, and watch things harmlessly whirling while we recovered a bit from the jet-lag. In other circumstances I might not have minded the badness of the film quite so much. But after three months in the earnest climate of Jerusalem we are not ready to let anything as feeble as this into our heads. It is a

case of cultural shock. The emptiness of the picture is sobering –
numbing. It gives me a sense of the rapid run of any number of
revolutions – egalitarian, sexual, aesthetic. They didn't last long
did they? They were serious, they were necessary but they were
very quickly bought to the boutique level. The great enemy of
progressive ideals is not the Establishment but the limitless
dullness of those who take them up.'

It sounds almost like Stoppard in *Travesties* condemning the
brevity of aesthetic revolutions and the vapidity of progressive
writers. But in the next decade Stoppard was to show that
Bellow's blast was somewhat premature.

Dirty Linen

It may or may not be significant that Stoppard went into
partnership with Clive Exton on a TV play, *The Boundary*.
Exton was the first dramatist to my knowledge ever to explore
the comic potential of a parliamentary sub-committee in a play
called *Have You Any Dirty Washing, Mother Dear?*, presented
at Hampstead Theatre in 1970. Stoppard became the second
dramatist to explore that field in *Dirty Linen* which started out
as a lunchtime *pièce d'occasion* at the Almost Free on April 6,
1976 and went on to have a long run at the Arts Theatre. The
starting-point was a celebration of the British naturalization of
Ed Berman, the bearded American-born dynamo behind the
Inter-Action Community group who had presented *Dogg's Our
Pet*. Stoppard's pen ran away with him and he ended up
incorporating another short play, *New-Found-Land*, into the
main work to reintroduce the American Connection.

Dirty Linen is Stoppard at his most festive, writing a pocket-
farce about a House of Commons Select Committee investigating
the sexual conduct of MPs and discovering that someone is
going through the massed ranks of MPs 'like a lawn-mower in
knickers.' The clerk assigned to the committee is one Maddie
Gotobed and it doesn't take more than a minute to realise that
she is the Mystery Woman who has been cutting a sexual swathe
through the lobbies and who has compromised most of the
committee members by dining with them at the Coq d'Or. Into
this, Stoppard inserts a playlet involving two Home Office
officials considering a naturalisation application by a bearded
American who has identical status to Mr Berman. Stoppard

yokes the two plays together by bringing on the Home Secretary who immediately vacates the room for the select committee and sanctions the naturalisation request when he recognises Maddie. It is a nice in-joke to think that Mr Berman might have become a True Brit because of the licentious behaviour of our rulers.

Stoppard likes farce; and he makes great play of jokes like items of female underwear emerging from the briefcases of the MPs and of the committee members struggling unsuccesfully to suppress their libidinous sub-conscious. Ronnie Barker (the original Birdboot in *The Real Inspector Hound*) does a familiar sketch in *The Two Ronnies* in which some respectable-looking figure allows his linguistic slips to show; and Stoppard uses precisely the same idea here as Cocklebury-Smythe MP stands transfixed by Maddie's cleavage:

> 'McTeazle, why don't you see if you can raise those great tits – boobs – those boobies, absolute tits don't you agree, Malcolm and Douglas – though good men as well, of course, useful chaps, very decent, first rate, two of the best, Malcolm and Douglas, why don't you have a quick poke, peek, in the Members' Bra – or the cafeteria, they're probably guzzling coffee and Swedish panties, (*Maddie has crossed her legs.*) Danish, I'll tell you what, why don't you go and see if you can raise Malcolm and Douglas . . .'

But along with the subliminal sex-talk, the farcical sight-gags, the verbal by-play about the Coq d'Or, the Golden Cock, the Old Clock and the Green Cockatoo (the kind of thing Ray Cooney does with equal facility), Stoppard is also making one or two serious points in the play about public morality and the snooping lubriciousness of the press. Britain has had its fair share of sex-scandals since the Sixties (Profumo, Lord Lambton, Cecil Parkinson) and it was one of these that prompted Peregrine Worsthorne incautiously to say on television that most people don't give a fuck about what MPs get up to in their spare time. That, more elegantly expressed, is the point of *Dirty Linen*; but the irony is that the mouthpiece of moral comment is Maddie who looks like a sexy, dumb blonde but who early on encapsulates the message: 'People don't care what MPs do in their spare time, they just want them to do their jobs properly bringing down prices and everything.' Stoppard neatly has it both ways making Maddie lose most of her outer garments – to cries of 'Strewth' and the flash of a camera – as the play proceeds and at the same time act as a spokesperson for common sense. What is significant is that Stoppard is – virtually for the first time – writing a play with a clear, unequivocal point-of-view. He is off the fence and into the arena.

Leftish British dramatists have a long-standing fascination with the sexual foibles of our politicians. Howard Brenton's *Fruit* dealt with a homosexually-inclined Conservative leader. Howard Barker's *Alpha, Alpha*, put the finger on a Labour Peer fascinated by gangland brutality and rough trade. G.F. Newman's *An Honourable Trade* in the 1980s suggested that many of our MPs were maladjusted masochists and impotent wrecks who enjoyed being dominated by a stern nanny-figure. The basic posture has been one of puritan dislike of the politicians, peers and judges who combine public rectitude with private fallibility. Stoppard, in total contrast, suggests that what MPs do in the bedroom is of no importance compared to what they get up to – or fail to get up to – in the Chamber.

Stoppard, the ex-journalist, also has a fair shy at the press claiming – again through the mouth of Maddie – that the more you accuse them of malice, the more you acknowledge their right to intrude into private lives; and, also, that most hacks are driven less by the urge to reveal truth than by the need to outdo their rivals' stories. It was true when Stoppard wrote the play in 1976. It is even more true ten years on when stories about the royals, sports stars, soap-opera luminaries occupy the front pages of the nastier end of Fleet Street. When no less than six reporters are employed by a paper to dig for dirt in the life of a famous cricketer, Ian Botham, as if he were a notorious murderer, our popular press has sunk to a dismal low. Stoppard in later plays went on to defend the ideal of press freedom: in *Dirty Linen* he shows how that abstract concept has been besmirched.

But he also has a good, parodic go at the quality papers and clearly enjoys puncturing their style. He gieves us a generous sample of a *The Times* leader (school of Rees-Mogg) filled with Latin tags and eloquent posturing: 'It needs no Gibbon come from the grave to spell out the danger to good government of a moral vacuum at the centre of power.' He also has a fair crack at the *Guardian's* ability to hit a note of worldly disdain, though its leader-writers are rather less prone to foreign phrases than

Stoppard implies. Stoppard's main point is that Fleet Street is riddled with hypocrisy, double-standards and moral attitudinising, and it is refreshing to find him using his knowledge of the real world.

Dirty Linen is a *divertissement* with a point of view: it is deft, funny and humane. For Stoppard-fanciers it also offers evidence of his governing preoccupations; and one of them is clearly that logic is manipulable and that words are prone to subjective coloration. Cocklebury-Smythe has been offered a Life Peerage by the PM but maintains that he is in line for a hereditary title and would rather be a real peer than a bogus one. The PM objects: '"Now look here, Cockie!" he said to me, "if they weren't real peers they wouldn't be in the House of Lords would they – that's logic." "If that's logic", I said, "you can turn a regimental goat into a Lieutenant Colonel by electing it to the United Services Club." "That's an interesting point, Cockie", he said. "It could explain a lot of my problems".' Under the gag, you sense Stoppard's lurking fascination with what, in life, is the real thing and with the way in which words mean different things depending on who is using them at the time.

I don't wish to load too much onto a lunchtime, occasional play. But *Dirty Linen* has some significance in that it shows Stoppard coming clean on a particular issue. It also shows him delighting (why not?) in his own virtuosity and writing a speech for the junior Home-Office official (delivered by Stephen Moore in the original production with rhapsodic fervour) that combines a coast-to-coast cliché vision of America with an astonishing sense of filigree detail: thus in Chicago 'Shirt-sleeved newspapermen of the old school throw in their cards in disgust and spit tobacco juice upon the well-shined shoes of anyone reading a New York paper.' That is like a freeze-frame image from *The Front Page*. And what you get throughout both the larger play – and the topographically colourful insert – is a firm sense of a point being made and Stoppard both enjoying farcical mechanics and sending language on a roller-coaster ride. *Dirty Linen* is worth being watched in public.

Every Good Boy Deserves Favour

Up to this point Stoppard's work had often been concerned with moral issues: questions of good and evil, right and wrong. The implication of his work is that life is so chaotic and confusing that the only way to cope with it is by detachment (Lord Malquist, Albert), retreat into a private world (Glad, John Brown) or panic-stricken cries for help (Dotty). Political action is rarely mentioned; and the idea that a work of art may itself grapple with socio-political issues or help in any way to change society is actively questioned in *Travesties*. From 1977 on we find a change in Stoppard's work and a persistent attempt to deal with human rights and the suppression of basic freedoms. It would be ludicrous to suggest that Stoppard underwent some overnight Pauline conversion: as someone born in Czechoslovakia, an ex-journalist and a more-than-intelligent human being (not mutually exclusive categories) he obviously was profoundly aware of what was happening in the Soviet bloc. If there was a change, it was in his attitude to the function of drama. In his interviews, there was an obvious awareness that he had mined a particular seam of heady extravaganza in *Jumpers* and *Travesties*. I believe that he had also used the latter play as a mind-clearing exercise to put the case for and against the social efficacy of art. There is no sign of him changing his endorsement of Auden's view that his poetry didn't save a single Jew from the gas-chambers. But Stoppard does at least seem to have accepted that there are some public issues so overpowering that they cannot be excluded from drama.

External circumstances also dictated Stoppard's choice of subject. As he himself records, he had promised to write a TV play to mark Amnesty International's Prisoner of Conscience Year (1977). To that end, he read books and articles by and about Russian dissidents and in 1976 met Victor Fainberg who had been arrested in Red Square in August, 1968 during a peaceful demonstration against the Warsaw Pact invasion of Czechoslovakia. Mr Fainberg had been declared insane and in 1974 emerged into exile from five years in the Soviet prison-hospital system. Stoppard's research into the plight of Russian dissidents coincided with a long-standing commission from André Previn to write a stage-piece demanding the presence of a live, full-size orchestra. Out of this conjunction of events came *Every Good Boy Deserves Favour* which was originally given what was intended as a one-off performance at the Royal Festival Hall on July 1, 1977. The piece is about a Russian dissident who is locked in a hospital cell with a real lunatic who believes himself to be in charge of an orchestra; and both the timeliness of the subject and the moral force of the piece have given it a long, much-performed life.

The first and obvious thing to say is that the play deals with a profoundly grim subject while retaining Stoppard's delight in bizarre conjunctions, ingenious wordplay, telling ironies (the dissident hero, Alexander, is constantly begged not to be so 'rigid') and outrageous jokes. Stoppard is not the first person – nor will he be the last – to handle a sombre theme with wit and irony. Joseph Heller's 1961 novel, *Catch-22*, dealt with the experiences of a Second World War bombardier with a tonic verbal gaiety. Stanley Kubrick's *Dr Strangelove* in 1963 satirised the military mentality and its capacity to despatch us all to nuclear oblivion in terms of cinematic farce. And shortly after Stoppard's play appeared Peter Barnes came up with an even more daring – though ultimately less durable – work called *Laughter* which treated the despotism of Ivan the Terrible and the horrors of Auschwitz as subjects too terrible to be dealt with in any other way than through comedy. What Stoppard does in *Every Good Boy*, however, is go beyond contrapuntal comic techniques. He stretches the brutal logic of the Soviet system – whereby political dissidents are treated as mental cases – so that it acquires an absurd dimension. He also, through his work, suggests there is an existence beyond demented barbarity. Robert Cushman put it well in his *Observer* review when he wrote: 'If a playwright wishes to fire us against injustice or the waste of life he must first convince us, in the quality of his own work, that life is worth living anyway. Mr Stoppard's gaiety is a moral quality in itself.'

Precisely so. But that gaiety is here anchored to a political purpose. In Audenesque terms, *Every Good Boy* may not have saved another dissident from persecution: what it did, through the medium of theatre, was to heighten our awareness *in a communal situation*. As a play, it also very effectively splices the jokes with intimations of horror, and the interrogations with an *Alice In Wonderland* craziness. Ivanov, who hears an orchestra in his head, shares a cell with Alexander, who is incarcerated for political purposes. Ivanov's complaints about his invisible orchestra – made all the funnier when backed up by the visible panoply of the London Symphony Orchestra – are typically Stoppardian: 'I've got a blue-arsed bassoon, a blue-tongued contra-bassoon, an organ grinder's chimpani and the bass drum is in urgent need of a dermatologist.' But as Ivanov desperately tries to discover what Alexander's instrument is he suddenly enquires, 'If I beat you to a pulp would you try to protect your face or your hands'. The very tone of the question implies that both men inhabit an unusually brutal society.

Stoppard's technique throughout is to destroy the barrier that divides the comic and the serious. Ivanov plays the triangle in his fantasy-band: Alexander's son, Sacha, is constantly quizzed about mathematical triangles. Ivanov imagines an orchestra: the Soviet Union is depicted as an orchestrated society. Ivanov is encouraged to banish his imaginary orchestra by a Doctor who plays the violin in a real orchestra and indeed emerges from the players on stage. Stoppard is not saying that jokes are the only way to deal with an appalling situation: he is saying that the Soviet situation has itself become a grim, ironic joke in which levels of reality have become a matter of arbitrary definition by the State. Stoppard's dialogue itself captures the bizarre way in which logic has been stood on its head. Alexander, for instance, complains that he is made to share a cell with a raving lunatic:

DOCTOR: Of course. The idea that all the people locked up in mental hospitals are sane while the people walking about outside are all mad is merely a literary conceit, put about by people who should be locked up. I assure you there's not much in it. Taken as a whole, the sane are out there and the sick are in here. For example, *you* are here because you have delusions, that sane people are put in mental hospitals.

ALEXANDER: But I *am* in a mental hospital.

DOCTOR: That's what I said. If you're not prepared to discuss your case rationally, we're going to go round in circles.

This is Lewis Carroll in the Soviet Union.

Running through the play is another very crucial point: that the Soviet Union craves acceptance in the modern world and does not want to be identified by its manifestations of cruelty. As Alexander says, 'If your name is known in the West, it is an embarrassment. The bad old days were over long ago. Things are different now. Russia is a civilised country, very good at Swan Lake and space technology, and it is confusing if people starve themselves to death.' Indeed, at the very heart of this charged, economical play is the conflict between Alexander's determination to cling to the truth that he is not mad and the pressures exerted upon him – by the Doctor and by his compassionate, indoctrinated son, Sacha – to end his rigidity and admit that he is a cured lunatic. Alexander defiantly cries:

'Dear Sacha try to see
What they call their liberty
is just the freedom to agree
that one and one is sometimes three.
I kiss you now, remember me.
Don't neglect your geometry.'

We would seem to have reached an impasse. But Stoppard resolves the situation: the two men locked up in the cell are both called Alexander Ivanov, when Colonel (or rather Doctor Rozinsky), who has made this arrangement arrives to interrogate them, he deliberately confuses them. He asks Ivanov if he believes sane people are put in mental hospitals and is told No; he asks Alexander if he has an orchestra and is again told No. Conclusion: 'There's absolutely nothing wrong with these men. Get them out of here.' Like many people seeing the first production at the Royal Festival Hall, I myopically concluded that the Colonel himself was acting out of confusion. Of course, the real point is that he has deliberately put the two prisoners together and knows full well what he is doing in asking them inappropriate questions. The ending of the play is thus not a happy one and Bernard Levin was wrong to conclude that it triumphantly says 'the gates of hell shall not prevail'. What it actually shows is the discharge both of a genuine lunatic (albeit a harmless one) and of a prisoner of conscience forced to bend the knee to a system he has knowingly defied. What happiness there is in the conclusion is purely ironic, in the manner of *The Threepenny Opera* where Macheath is saved from the gallows by a fortuitous, improbable beneficience.

Stoppard's play is not, of course, the whole truth or indeed the only truth about the Soviet Union; and I think we should beware of the anti-Soviet fundamentalists who seize upon it as if it were. In the course of two, admittedly brief, visits to the Soviet Union I have at least managed to grasp the point that it is a vast, bewilderingly diverse country and that any generalisation about it can be quickly cancelled out by another. To someone like myself fascinated by its architecture, its landscape, its culture, its ungovernable variety, what is most dismaying is the hysterical insecurity it manifests in its treatment of dissidents: the poet Irina Ratushinskaya (now released from the 'strict regime' camp where she was incarcerated) was, for instance, warned even before her arrest by the KGB that her poems were a threat to the security of the Soviet Union, that they undermined the Soviet regime, and that the Soviet regime had no option but to defend itself against them. Those of us who argue against the demonological view of the Soviet Union that prevails in much of the West are left helpless by such behaviour.

What Stoppard has written here is far from being a crude piece of anti-Soviet propaganda: it is too springy and alert for that. What it does say is that the Soviet authorities have lost touch with their own mortality and there is an *Alice in Wonderland* surreality about a system in which political dissent is treated as a form of madness while certifiable madness is treated with bone-headed incomprehension. Its significance in terms of Stoppard's development is that it shows him allying his mathematical mind and verbal cleverness to his moral passion: it proves that, to the true artist, convictions are not prisons.

Professional Foul

This play, transmitted on BBC Television on September 24, 1977, confirms the point. It is, I believe, the best play Stoppard had written at this stage of his career. One reason is that it shows a Cambridge Professor of Ethics confronting the real world of persecution and modifying his whole philosophy to recognise that there is such a thing as an instinctive morality based on right and wrong: he goes to Prague to lecture on 'Ethical Fictions as Ethical Foundations', and to see a football match, and returns home 'educated by experience' to use Stoppard's own words. Another reason is that the play is a very sophisticated structure offering endless ironic reflections on the title with its reference to pragmatic, ethically questionable actions committed in pursuit of a goal. A third reason is that the play works inside the naturalistic format demanded by television which makes it accessible and easy to apprehend like a very good thriller with a moral kick to it.

This last is a strictly personal point of view; and many people who work inside TV drama and film lament the confining realism of the form. I happen to think it suits Stoppard particularly well. TV drama imposes the discipline of length. It also forces writers to create plausible people doing plausible things in a plausible situation. Stoppard's strength as a writer is the brilliance of his mind and the gaiety of his spirit: his weakness is a tendency to let things spiral out of control and to get seduced by his own cleverness. TV drama is a medium that has to communicate instantly to millions of people and is somewhat inimical to verbal pyrotechnics. Just as convictions are not prisons, so the seeming constraints of TV drama can be liberating; and in *Professional Foul* Stoppard creates a work that is realistic in setting, emotional in impact, beautifully-wrought in structure and deeply moral in intention. It works on sight but repays endless re-readings.

Stoppard himself says in his introduction that a week's visit to Moscow and Leningrad with a friend in February, 1977 paradoxically unlocked a play about Czechoslovakia. But his home-country had clearly been on his mind; especially after the arrest in Prague on January 6th of three men attempting to deliver a document, Charter '77, that requested the government to implement its own laws in accord with the Helsinki agreements. Stoppard himself visited Prague in June of that year and wrote memorably about the Chartists in the *New York Review of Books*. *Professional Foul* pre-dates that and is not, in any sense, a documentary about Prague but a play about the primacy of instinctive ethical responses. In it we see Anderson, a Cambridge Professor of Ethics, going to Prague to deliver a paper at a philosophical colloquium and to watch England play soccer in a World Cup qualifier. In the course of the trip he meets a former student – Pavel Hollar – who asks him to take back to England a thesis on 'correct behaviour' and get it translated. Anderson temporarily accepts the package. The next day he goes to Hollar's flat to return it only to find that Hollar has been arrested and that his flat is being searched by the secret police. Shaken by what he has seen, Anderson subsequently changes his speech on ethics to the colloquium making a direct plea for a consensus on individual rights. He also smuggles the crucial thesis back to England via the luggage of a colleague who regards himself as a bit of a neo-Marxist and moral pragmatist. As they fly off, Anderson concludes, 'Ethics is a very complicated business. That's why they have these congresses.'

What makes this a brilliant play is that Anderson's education-in-life is worked out in terms of a plot that is superbly constructed without being offensively rigged. The first scene, for instance, on the flight into Prague, establishes many things: the suspect irrelevance of an event called 'Colloquium Philosophicum Prague '77' (first seen on the cover of a glossy brochure) at a time when those demanding human rights are being arrested; the comfortably-cushioned world of the academic jaunt (fully satirised later by Malcolm Bradbury in *Rates of Exchange* and David Lodge in *Small World*); the finicky precision of Anderson who collects 'little curiosities for the language chaps' in his notebook; the marginal interest in their host-country shown both by Anderson, who talks of 'some rather dubious things' happening in Czechoslovakia, and by McKendrick, a colleague from Stoke, whose field is the philosophical assumptions of social science, and who sails pretty close to the wind, Marx-wise; the contrast between sex and the cerebrum with Anderson rather guiltily hiding a girlie-magazine under his lunch-tray and then having another one (vital to the plot) thrust upon him by McKendrick. But possibly the biggest hint as to what is to come is the lofty attitude shown by these two academics to a third, emplaned colleague, Chetwyn, who take an Augustinian line on ethics and who writes letters to *The Times* about persecuted professors. With the deftness of an Ed McBain or a John D. Macdonald, Stoppard establishes most of the clues for the later drama.

Stoppard gets to the meat of the drama when Anderson is confronted in his hotel room by Pavel Hollar, who did doctoral studies in Paine and Locke but who is now forced to clean lavatories. Anderson is well-meaning and precise but shows a total lack of empathy with Pavel's plight and bows out of smuggling his thesis on 'correct behaviour' out of the country on the grounds it would compromise his status as a government-guest. But the whole scene (indeed the whole play) is about the very question of what correct behaviour is. Pavel's argument is that 'The ethics of the State must be judged against the fundamental ethic of the individual. The human being, not the citizen.' For Anderson, this is a matter for nice debate rather than instant acceptance: he treats it as if it were an essay from a student:

> 'The difficulty arises when one asks oneself how the *individual* ethic can have any meaning by itself. Where does *that* come from? In what sense is it intelligible, for example, to say that a man has certain inherent, individual rights? It is much easier to understand how a community of individuals can decide to give each other certain rights. These rights may or may not include, for example, the right to publish something. In that situation, the individual ethic would flow from the collective ethic, just as the State says it does.'

The stunning irrelevance of Anderson's arguments, in the particular situation, is underlined by Stoppard by the way in which the conversation has to be conducted first in the corridor and then in the bathroom with the taps running for fear of bugging. The point is underlined (and the plot furthered) by the fact that Pavel dare not take his thesis with him in case he is arrested and so leaves it in Anderson's briefcase on the assumption he can return it the next day. The kind of philosophical arguments we heard in *Jumpers* are here placed against a background of political reality.

Football interweaves deftly with philosophy (both, incidentally preoccupations of A.J. Ayer – though there the resemblance with Anderson ends). Anderson's ethical precepts may be theoretical but his knowledge of soccer is extremely practical: meeting two English soccer-stars in the hotel lift he gives them unheeded advice about watching for the danger of the short corner and the chip to the far post by the tall Jirasek. Stoppard also gets maximum comic mileage out of McKendrick's mistaking the soccer-players for philosophers and asking whether they're going to the open forums by neo-Hegelians or Quinian neo-Positivists. Stoppard even shows us part of the Colloquium with an American academic wittering on about semantic confusion. Point taken; but what is fascinating is how Stoppard uses the scene to add to the thematic density of the play: when Anderson is caught in the spotlight – sneaking out

118

first to return Pavel's thesis and then go to the soccer-match – he has to offer an instant gloss on the American's waffle and comes up with the devastating point that the importance of language is overrated and that 'the important truths are simple and monolithic'. He says it but he doesn't yet act on it.

Stoppard himself does. As a dramatist he has tended hitherto to pull back on the brink of depicting real pain, real anguish: even in *Every Good Boy* Alexander *describes* the process of his arrest and locking-up. Here, Stoppard shirks nothing. When Anderson arrives at the Hollar apartment he finds himself in the midst of an extensive police-search, he himself is detained as Mrs Hollar's witness and yet, even when confronted by the reality of Czech police-tactics, he is mainly concerned with the threat to his own liberty. He is concerned with missing a soccer-match even while his friend's apartment is being ransacked. But Stoppard keeps the football parallels alive. On the radio we hear that Broadbent, the 'opportunist' English centre, has committed a professional foul: the police do the same in 'discovering' a pack of American dollars under the floorboards. If anything breaks through Anderson's moral detachment it is the sight of Mrs Hollar's ten-year-old son, Sacha, comforting his mother as though he were a small adult. That is the Aristotelian turning-point of the whole drama.

But Stoppard, good dramatist that he is, doesn't immediately make us aware of the effect of all this on Anderson. Back at the hotel, he gives us a dead-accurate scene of two journalists dictating match-reports to their papers (one pop, one posh). He also, in a hotel dining-room scene, extends the play's philosophic ideas. McKendrick explores his idea that a moral principle is not indefinitely extendible and does not hold good for any situation. He argues that Morality and Immorality are not parallel lines on separate planes:

'They're the edges of the same plane – it's in three dimensions, you see – and if you twist the plane in a certain way, into what we call the catastrophe curve, you get a model of the sort of behaviour we find in the real world. There's a point – the catastrophe point – where your progress along one line of behaviour jumps you into the opposite line; the principle reverses itself at the point where a rational man would abandon it.'

So Chetwyn believes in God-given absolutes of goodness and beauty; Anderson in ethical fictions which determine our behaviour; and McKendrick in a slippery notion of moral reversal. Again, Stoppard deepens and extends his argument on correct behaviour and goes on to contrast philosophical theory with human practice.

Anderson meets with Mrs Hollar and Sacha in a park. As Robert Cushman pointed out, it is a scene that goes deeper emotionally than anything Stoppard has written before. What is fascinating is Stoppard's use of the child – as in *Every Good Boy* – to draw our sympathy (why not?) and make clear the forced maturity of children in an oppressive state. Technically, it is also important that Stoppard still delays the full revelation of Anderson's change of heart and mind: he simply agrees to hand back the thesis to a friend of Hollar's at the congress while saying he will use his influence back home to secure Pavel's release.

What is good about this play is that no scene is wasted. Everything contributes to the central idea. What is correct behaviour? Are the ethics of the group determined by the ethics of the individual? Back at the hotel there is a wonderful scene where a drunk McKendrick confronts the footballers and reporters and gets involved in a heated debate as to whether the behaviour of soccer-crowds is determined by that on the field. 'How can you,' he asks, 'expect the kids to be little gentlemen when their heroes behave like yobs – answer me that – no – you haven't answered my question – if you've got yobs on the fields you're going to have yobs on the terraces.' Of course, the scene is very funny. But it is another crucial extension of the central debate about the source of ethical principles and it ends with a crisp pay-off when Broadbent admits that Anderson was right about the Czech footballer Jirasek but cruelly adds, 'They don't teach you nothing at that place then'. To which Anderson simply replies 'No.'

Anderson's moral conversion is only made clear next day at the Colloquium when he abandons his prepared, already circulated paper on Ethical Fictions and instead addresses himself to 'the conflict between the rights of individuals and the rights of the community'. Anderson's basic point is that communities have rules but that these are a secondary and consequential elaboration of primary rights. There may be argument as to whether those primary human rights are the

120

result of collective decisions or as the endowment of God, but that matters less than the fact that there is a broad agreement on those human rights. Anderson (in a sense committing a professional foul by not delivering the scheduled paper and causing panic to his Chairman) goes on:

'What strikes us is the consensus about an individual's rights put forward by those who invoke God's authority and by those who invoke no authority at all other than their own idea of what is fair and sensible. The first Article of the American Constitution, guaranteeing freedom of religious observance, of expression, of the press, and of assembly, is closely echoed by Articles 28 and 32 of the no less admirable Constitution of Czechoslovakia, our generous hosts on this occasion. Likewise protection from invasion of privacy, from unreasonable search and from interference with letters and correspondence guaranteed to the American people by Article 4 is likewise guaranteed to the Czech people by Article 31.'

Not only does Anderson use Colloquium Prague '77 to state the basic principles of Charter '77. He has come round eloquently to the view that there is a broad, universal agreement as to the nature of human rights. He, then, bravely, goes much further and examines the source of individual ethics, qualifying the linguists' view that ethics are merely the creation of our utterances. He comes to the conclusion that 'There is a sense of right and wrong which precedes utterance. It is individually experienced and it concerns one person's dealings with another person. From this experience we have built a system of ethics which is the sum of individual acts of recognition of individual right.' Echoing Matthew Arnold's point that the State is simply the individual raised to the highest power, he suggests that when the State ethic finds itself in conflict with the individual ethic then the results are illogical, embarrassing and an exposure of the totalitarian fallacy. Which, of course, is precisely what Pavel Hollar was arguing in the first place. And, as we see, the only way the State can cope with this onslaught on its methods is by abruptly terminating the proceedings through a false fire alarm.

Stoppard's final pay-off comes at the airport and on the plane home. Three philosophers flew into Prague 48 hours before. Two leave it. Chetwyn, the moral absolutist, has been held by the authorities for carrying letters to Amnesty International and the UN. Anderson, the calculating proponent of human rights, has been stopped because of a suspicious bulge in his suitcase which turns out to be McKendrick's girlie-magazine. McKendrick, the soft Marxist and moral pragmatist, has sailed through the airport-checks carrying, unbeknownst to him, Pavel's subversive thesis. Anderson has committed the final professional foul and hoist McKendrick with his own petard by reversing a moral principle. Ethics is indeed a complicated business.

I have dealt with this play in detail because it shows Stoppard achieving a new level of skill. He takes a popular, almost thriller, format and injects into it a debate about the gap between public and private morality, philosophy and practice, individual and collective ethics in debased systems; about the nature of justice, the maturity of youth, about the way professional fouls can be either counter-productive or beneficial depending on circumstances. It is a play about philosophy, football and moral courage. It is also a classically constructed play in which the innocent hero acquires knowledge, experiences a spiritual turning-point and emerges purified. At a deeper level, it also asks how long a system can survive when it is based on illogic and a denial of human rights. The answer, in practice, would seem to be a very long time indeed.

The heartening thing is that Stoppard, who once said on the TV programme *One Pair of Eyes* that 'I should have the courage of my lack of convictions', here emerges as a man of very strong convictions indeed. For the third play running, he makes it perfectly clear where he stands; and not by turning the characters into spokesmen for himself but through the logical and plausible development of the dramatic action. His quondam brilliance has here been harnessed to a moral and political purpose; and his playwriting is all the better for it.

Night and Day

Naturalism has become a rather dirty word in the theatre. But we should remind ourselves that as a literary-theatrical movement it dates back to the 1880s and has been the source of most of the worthwhile drama of the last 100 years: without it there would be no Ibsen, Chekhov, Shaw, Schnitzler, O'Casey, Miller or Williams. Émile Zola wrote a prefatorial manifesto to his stage

122

adaptation of *Thérèse Räquin* which sounded the trumpet-note and made clear the historical necessity of the movement:

> 'I am absolutely convinced that we shall next see the Naturalist movement imposed on the theatre and bringing to it the power of reality, the new life of modern art. The drama dies unless it is rejuvenated by new life. We must put new blood into this corpse . . . I defy the last of the Romantics to put upon the stage a heroic drama: at the sight of all the paraphernalia of armour, secret doors, poisoned wines and the rest, the audience would only shrug its shoulders. And melodrama, that middle-class off-spring of the romantic drama, is in the hearts of the people more dead than its predecessor; its false sentiment, its complication of stolen children and discovered documents have finally rendered it despicable so that any attempt to revive it proves abortive . . . the experimental and scientific spirit of the century will enter the domain of the drama, and in this lies the only possible salvation of the drama . . . we must look to the future and the future will have to do with the human problem studied in the framework of reality. The drama will either die or become modern and realistic.'

Naturalism was an idealistic movement directly connected with the increasing urbanisation and mechanisation of life, democratic reformism, a concern with the condition of the people, and the development of the physical sciences which aimed at controlling nature by knowing its processes.

I state this because many people greeted Stoppard's *Night and Day* (which had its première at London's Phoenix Theatre on November 8, 1978) as a descent into naturalism after the turbulent extravagance of works like *Jumpers* and *Travesties*. I admit that the naturalism of Stoppard may have as much to do with a well-carpentered theatricality as with the kind of questing experimentalism envisaged by Zola, but there is nothing wrong with naturalism *per se*. In *Night and Day* Stoppard offers us a commercially-produced play that presents a multi-layered, if sometimes loaded, debate on freedom. He laces the naturalism (as most dramatists do) with non-naturalistic devices. He also creates in Ruth Carson, the bored wife of a mining engineer, his most credible, closely-observed female character to date. It may not be Stoppard's finest play; but it is provocative, needling and written from the heart as well as the head.

When it opened at the Phoenix most critics (myself included) treated it largely as a debate about press freedom. Steve Grant in *Plays and Players* was the first critic to point out that it consists of three interlocking layers, all of which are concerned with freedom. There is the central debate on the freedom of the press raising the question of who is best equipped to run newspapers; there is the romantic predicament of Ruth Carson, married to a stable, decent man but yearning for sexual freedom and independence; and there is the political turmoil of the fictitious African state of Kimbabwe which is independent, emergent but neither free from strife nor from the vested economic interests of the big powers. If the play has any kind of moral, it is that freedom is a heady condition; but also one that bring with it responsibilities, problems, external and internal conflicts.

Stoppard sets the action in Kimbabwe at a time of incipient civil war between the dictatorial, Charterhouse and London School of Economics – educated President Mageeba and the secessionist Colonel Shimbu who is head of the Adoma Liberation Front and who has seized control of the country's economically vital, copper-producing mines. The setting is the rich, neo-colonial house of a British mining-engineer, Geoffrey Carson, and his acerbically intelligent second wife, Ruth, who was once feverishly pursued by Fleet Street hacks in a society divorce case. The house is temporarily invaded by a posse of British jouranlists: Guthrie, a tough, battle-wise Don McCullin-type photographer, Wagner an Australian-born visiting fireman who works for a prestigious Sunday paper, *The Globe*, and Milne, an idealistic freelance who lost his job on a Grimsby paper because of his anti-union stance and who, when the play begins, has scooped Wagner in his own paper with an exclusive, front-page interview with Colonel Shimbu. Not only are Wagner and Milne ethical and professional rivals: they are sexual rivals too since Wagner has slept with Ruth Carson in London and now she is profoundly stirred by the attractive Milne. In the play, Milne looks like scooping Wagner for a second time when he and Guthrie drive off to meet Shimbu bearing a message from Mageeba. However, Wagner the hardened pro, realises the real story is happening back at the Carson home where Mageeba is due to arrive for a breakfast showdown with his secessionist rival. In driving through the enemy lines, Milne is killed. Wagner gets both a lip-smacking interview, and a sound beating, from

Mageeba. But, having earlier despatched a telex complaining about the use of copy by the blackleg Milne, he is hoist with his own petard when he finds a chapel protest has shut the paper down for that weekend. He files a quick obit. on Milne and retires to bed with Ruth Carson.

This is a play with a beginning, a middle and an end; and for once in Stoppard they are in that order. It is also a play about definitions of freedom working on three different, inter-related levels. But in the central journalistic section what strikes me is how Stoppard gets some (not all) of the tone and style right while giving us a one-eyed view of the press freedom v closed-shop debate. Stoppard has enough knowledge of the trade to deal accurately with the nuts and bolts: the slavering delight at the sight of a telex-machine, the frantic concern with catching the Saturday-deadline, the joshing relationship (based on guarded mutual respect) between writer and photographer, the insensate fury at being gazumped on one's very own front page. Stoppard also indulges in one of his favourite sports: journalistic parody. Early on in the play, Wagner quotes extracts from the Sunday papers on the Zimbabwe story. Stoppard catches precisely the difference between *The Observer* which sees the peasant army of the ALF as having the 'tacit support of the indigenous population of the interior' and *The Sunday Telegraph* which sees the civilian population of the Adoma region as being intimidated into supporting 'the Russian-equipped rural guerillas of the ALF'. But he goes oddly astray in his parody of *The New York Times* swathed in mythic metaphor, 'In them thar hills to the north west, the renegade Colonel Shimbu is given no more chance than Colonel Custer – if only he'd stand still. Unfortunately no-one can find the Colonel to tell him to stop playing the Indians and it may be that Jeddu is going to wake up one morning with its armoured cars drawn up in a circle.' Since *New York Times* reporting is characterised by a factually-based sobriety – with little room for jokey colloquialism or extravagant colour – that rings strangely false.

What undermines the debate on press-freedom is Stoppard's determination tha the boy (or girl) in his corner should win: the essence of first-rate theatrical debate (vide Shaw) is that you pitch two perfectly-matched heavyweights against each other. Here Stoppard pits the idealistic Milne against the tough, union-supporting Wagner and treats the former as ethically superior.

Milne pours scorn on the jargon of the house-Trots, derides the notion that newspapers, national and local, are vast profit-making concerns and has a notable capper with the point that there is no god-given reason why printers shouldn't earn more than journalists when you look at the trite trash many of them are asked to set. To complete the rout of Wagner, a message comes through on the telex congratulating Milne on his exclusive interview with Shimbu.

It is worth looking in a bit more detail, however, at the arguments deployed. Milne has refused to join a provincial reporters' strike, has helped the management get the paper out, has subsequently been expelled by the union and refused to appeal against his expulsion and has then resigned when a majority of the journalists have refused to work with him and threatened to shut the paper down again. I would call such a man bloody-minded rather than high-principled. The real point is that Stoppard gives us no details of the cause of the original strike and therefore no chance of judging the ethical basis of Milne's actions. We are asked to applaud him purely because he took an anti-union line; but this seems to me knee-jerk Tebbitism. Milne also attacks Wagner's defence of worker-solidarity ('I bet they don't come much more solid than you') and then goes on to argue that there is no logical reason why printers shouldn't be paid more than journalists given some of the rubbish they are asked to print. But Milne's argument is self-defeating. Printers are not paid more than journalists as a value-judgement on the quality of the prose they are asked to set. They are paid more precisely because of union-muscle and the 'worker solidarity' Milne so despises.

The debate on press-freedom is extended later in the act in exchanges between Milne and Ruth. It is good writing in that Milne's idealistic fervour acts as a sexual magnet to the increasingly aroused Ruth. It's less good in that Milne puts arguments into the absent Wagner's mouth and then demolishes them and in that an artifical division is created between a free press and a journalists' closed-shop. In fact, a closed-shop in journalism is no more sinister than it is in acting, law or medicine. It is a means of ensuring there are minimum professional standards for qualification and of preventing managements from hiring casual labour. The real stumbling-block in *Night and Day* is that Milne, as Stoppard's acknowledged mouthpiece, is never pressed into defining his terms. He says 'No matter how imperfect things are, if you've got a free press everything is correctable and without it everything is concealable.' Stoppard has said 'I believe that to be a true statement. Milne has my prejudice if you like.' As a general aphorism, it is only true so long as Stoppard ignores the pressures on press-freedom that come from interventionist proprietors, strong-minded print unions (who refuse to set copy they find politically objectionable), the Official Secrets Act, lacklustre editors, government secrecy, the stringent libel laws. Obviously press freedom is a sacred ideal; obviously the British press is freer than most, but there are daily, visible pressures on that freedom (of the kind David Hare and Howard Brenton subsequently dealt with in *Pravda*) that neither Milne nor Stoppard acknowledges. Milne ventures the aphorism that 'Junk journalism is the evidence of a society that has got at least one thing right, that there should be nobody with the power to dictate where responsible journalism begins.' I offer the counter-proposition that: 'Junk journalism is proof of a society that has got one thing wrong which is that crude proprietorial power should be a licence for factual distortion, political bias and moral hypocrisy.'

Night and Day, in its different versions, nevertheless, offers proof that Stoppard listens to criticism without altering his basic principles. The point was made (by myself and others) that the second-act argument between Wagner and Ruth about who should own the papers was theatrically rigged, and that it was nonsense to argue that we had a richly diverse press pushing every available line when the national press was dominated by a Conservative political viewpoint. Stoppard had the grace to modify this by putting the defence of our press's diversity in the form of a reported conversation between Ruth and her eight-year-old son, and by allowing Wagner to state that the press is still basically in the hands of the big barons. Even the revised argument has now become dated. New technology means that it is now cheaper to set up, print and distribute a newspaper and that the promised era of diversity should be upon us. Even so, Fleet Street's latest paper, *The Independent*, has cost £18 million to set up; and, although its investors are said to be more interested in profits than policies, one is free to ask how long that detachment would survive if the paper made a substantial loss. 'Information is light,' says Guthrie in the course of the play.

Most journalists would drink to that. But what Stoppard never really acknowledges – unlike the authors of *Pravda* – are the numerous filters that distort that light on its way to the newspaper-reader.

Ruth Carson eloquently defends press-freedom in general while deploring the Lego-set language of the pop papers and the intrusive antics of reporters. But while declaring that 'freedom is neutral' she enjoys less of it than anyone in the play (except the house-boy Francis). She is beautiful, intelligent, witty but, as a neo-colonial wife, she has no profession in which to exercise her talents; and even the flickerings of sexual desire are accompanied by remorse. Many of Stoppard's previous women characters (Jane Moon, Penelope, Dotty) have been dangerously attractive. Stoppard has at last written a female character from her own point of view rather than as part of a moral scheme; and he has even given her an internal voice sending out constant signals of desperation.

Ruth's problem is that she enjoys the normal stirrings of desire but is part of a class and a society where fidelity (in women anyway) is prized and monogamy practised. She is also self-aware enough to articulate her problem and that of myriad women everywhere as she explains to Wagner:

'Every now and again we meet a man who attracts us and we run a mile. I let you take me to dinner because there was no danger of going to bed with you. And then because there was no danger of going to bed with you a second time, I went to bed with you. A lady, if surprised by melancholy, might go to bed with a chap once; or a thousand times if consumed by passion. But twice, Wagner, *twice* . . . a lady might think she'd been taken for a tart.'

Ruth is bound by social conventions, moral scruples, the restrictions of the well-to-do wife in a post-colonial world: she actually sees herself like Elizabeth Taylor in *Elephant Walk* or Deborah Kerr in *King Solomon's Mines*. What is interesting is that Stoppard, who has hitherto kept passion out of his plays, here at last grapples with the prickly, unpredictable, dangerous quality of love. He makes it clear at the end of the first act that Ruth is smitten by Milne as he talks about press-freedom. At the start of the second act he writes a fantasy-sequence in which Ruth makes her passion for Milne obvious and in which she describes the state of quickened excitement she feels at his very presence:

> 'Went to bed feeling nothing more dangerous than a heightened sense of you being in the house. Woke up fluttering with imminent risk. Quite a pleasant feeling, really. Like walking along the top-board knowing you don't have to jump. But a desperate feeling too, because if you're not going to jump what the hell are you doing up there? So I got dressed to say goodbye to you. Really. Dressed for it.'

Stoppard writes an unreal scene in real, perfectly plausible dialogue. Indeed the audience in the theatre – coming back from the interval – is not quite sure on what level to take the scene. The pay-off comes when, at the end of it Milne walks up-stage into darkness, Ruth apparently following him, stepping out of her dress as she does so, watched by her husband who enters the room unhurriedly and looks after her. Then we hear the voice of the real Ruth from the sofa asking 'Got a cigarette?' And when Carson says 'You got dressed up for him' we feel a slight quiver of apprehension until we realise he means the President. Stoppard's technique has now matured to the point where he can lob a wish-fulfilment scene into a naturalistic play and yet leave us feeling at the end that Ruth's husband is perceptive enough to have guessed at his wife's desires. Ruth is a real character; and it says much for the role that it could accommodate actresses as diverse as Diana Rigg, who has a wonderfully keen, witty, apprehension like Shakespeare's Beatrice, and Maggie Smith who turns insecurity into a style and who endowed the role with her own particular brand of wristy, comic anguish.

The freedom-issue is given another twist in the play by the tumult in Kambabwe. Nominally it is a free, independent African state, but President Mageeba is a product of the British educational system and is still dependent on the expertise of a man like Geoffrey Carson to manage the copper, manganese and potash industry: his rival Colonel Shimbu is equally dependent, in order to carry out his secessionist raids, on a Russian-built airstrip and on Cuban pilots flying Mi-8 helicopters. Freedom in African states is, Stoppard implies, a relative business; and he turns that into a dangerous joke when the dictatorial President

Mageeba explains how he replaced the colonially-run newspaper whose premises burned down during the state of emergency. What to put in its place? He didn't want a state-run propaganda sheet nor the scepticism of a private-enterprise organ; and a democratic committee of journalists was out of the question:

> MAGEEBA: No, no – freedom without responsibility, that was the elusive formula we pondered all those years ago at the LSE. And that is what I found. From the ashes there arose, by public subscription, a new *Daily Citizen*, responsible and relatively free. Do you know what I mean by a relatively free press, Mr Wagner?
> WAGNER: Not exactly, sir, no.
> MAGEEBA: I mean a free press which is edited by one of my relatives.

At which point Mageeba laughs and brings the weighted end of his stick down on Wagner's head.

Admittedly the Mageeba scene presents a slight problem in that, as Stoppard conceded in an interview, 'When I write an African President into a play I have to contrive to make him the only African President who speaks like me.' And although Mageeba is slotted neatly into the play's intellectual scheme, there is something a bit improbable about him standing back politely listening while Ruth and Wagner have an intellectual ding-dong about the ownership of the press in a Western democracy. What Stoppard does finally suggest is that freedom is a concept that has different resonances and meanings depending on who is using the word and where they are standing. Freedom in the West implies the sanctity of basic institutions including the press. Freedom for Ruth implies freedom to fulfil her talents and to escape from the naggings of her conscience. Freedom in an African state implies some kind of compromise between the democratic and the autocratic pattern and is probably unrealisable until such states cease to be pawns in super-power strategies. Stoppard intertwines all these ideas and, at the close, shows the African war converging with the petty wars of Fleet Street while Ruth makes a small bid for some kind of personal freedom.

Those who like the Stoppard who turns intellectual cartwheels tend to look down on *Night and Day*: those of us who believe that much of the earlier work is dazzling but detached from human pain and passion tend to like it more. My own criticism of this play stems not from its naturalistic form but from the fact that Stoppard never truly challenges the idealistic, good-looking, martyred Milne and accepts too readily the notion that anyone who withstands union pressure must be a hero. Ironically Stoppard, so often criticised for his lack of convictions, here seems weighed down by them. The best features of the play are that it deals with sexual passion and desperation, that it dovetails its various treatments of freedom and that it shows you can take a one-set, eight-character commercial work and make it a vehicle for intelligent ideas. Only those regularly subjected to the trivial pursuits of West End theatre may realise how significant that is.

5

Cricket Bats and Passion

Stoppard, by now in his early 40s, had written four full length
plays. All had been hits. Inevitably this made him the focus of
admiration and envy, acclaim and sniping especially from
fellow-dramatists. The British cannot stand success so Stoppard
inevitably came in for his share of denigration. It seems a good
moment to pause and take an objective look at his strengths and
weaknesses as a writer.

Stoppard's major contribution to modern British drama thus
far was to help demolish the barrier between serious and fun
theatre. We tend to assume there is a certain tone and style you
adopt for the discussion of major issues such as human rights,
moral sanctions, the importance of art, press-freedom: there is
another tone and style you adopt for boulevard plays about
adultery and the vagaries of human affection. Other writers,
such as Peter Nichols in *A Day in the Death of Joe Egg* and
Alan Bennett in *Forty Years On* had done pathfinding work in
bringing the style of music-hall and revue to the discussion of
private tragedy and national decline; but Stoppard, as much as
anyone, proved that heavyweight topics could be approached
with gaiety of spirit. Laurence Olivier once said that theatre is
'the first glamouriser of thought.' Those words apply perfectly to
Stoppard. He glamourises thought. Some argue that he flatters
audiences into thinking they are cleverer than they are: at his
best, what he does is to extend an audience's interests and make
them more curious about the subjects he tackles.

Another prime virtue is his willingness to experiment with
form in whatever medium he is working in. Even in a naturalistic
stage play like *Night and Day* he introduces an equivocal
element of dream-like fantasy. In radio plays like *Albert's
Bridge* and *Artist Descending a Staircase* he utilises either aural
perspective or time-structures without lapsing into the ear-
bending self-indulgence of stereophonic drama with nothing to

say. Every dramatist carves out his own thematic territory. What draws us back to a writer, with constantly renewed interest, is his use of differing formal devices. I see a parallel, in fact, between Stoppard and the American composer-lyricist Stephen Sondheim. Sondheim musicals exhibit a continuing fascination with loneliness, despair, mortality, the barrenness of modern society; but the striking thing about *Follies*, *Pacific Overtures*, *Merrily We Roll Along*, *Sunday in the Park with George* is how Sondheim's fundamental pessimism finds new forms in each show.

Stoppard is a populariser, a glamouriser, an adventurer. What he lacked, at this stage in his career, was the capacity to make us care very deeply about his characters or even to portray their inmost emotions. John Osborne once described his own plays as 'lessons in feeling': Stoppard's are lessons in thinking. Salutary as that is, one can't help regretting the dearth of modern British plays that deal with raw, undiluted, unashamed passion: the kind unearthed by Eugene O'Neill in *Long Day's Journey Into Night*. American drama generally seems much closer to people's emotional core; and one reason I suspect for the popularity of playwrights like David Mamet and Sam Shepard is that they don't come armed with concepts but with baffled, struggling, helpless, sometimes inarticulate characters. Drama of ideas and drama of character are not mutually exclusive. The weakness of British drama since the war has been that irony, articulacy, cleverness, polemic and sheer point-scoring have frequently replaced a fascination with common human joys and sufferings. Stoppard, as much as anyone, has often seemed to conceal his basic humanity under his palpable cleverness. His delight in what makes us eccentrically different has prevented him dealing with the qualities that unite us. The question, as one examines his most recent work, is whether he could bring intellect and passion into simultaneous play.

Undiscovered Country

An affirmative answer was provided by a play Stoppard didn't so much create as recreate: *Undiscovered Country*. This was the third time Stoppard had worked on a version of a play in a language he didn't speak. In 1965 he was called in, at a late stage, to render Nicholas Bethell's translation of Mrozek's

Tango for the RSC more readily speakable. In 1973, working from a literal translation by Katie Kendall, he came up with a fresh version of Lorca's *The House of Bernarda Alba* for Robin Phillips at Greenwich Theatre. Now in 1979, working this time from a literal translation by John Harrison, he wrote a 'version' of Arthur Schnitzler's *Das Weite Land* called *Undiscovered Country*: one there for Lord Malquist and his monograph on titles deriving from *Hamlet*.

In theory, the idea of dramatists producing 'versions' of plays in languages they don't speak is indefensible. The audience can't be sure whether it is getting the original text or the original overlaid with the style of a living author. The standard defence is that an experienced playwright can come up with a flexibly speakable version that doesn't sound like a translation. I hold to the slightly unfashionable view that, when you encounter an English version of a foreign classic, it *should* sound like a translation. I would rather have an accurate account of the first author's text than something racily 'speakable': when I go to Racine in English I want to hear the insistent beat of the Alexandrines. Ideally, of course, what is best is the work of foreign dramatists translated by people (like Christoper Hampton and Michael Frayn) who are both fluent linguists and accomplished dramatists. Even here, a certain self-effacement is required: when Tony Harrison renders *Phèdre* as *Phaedra Britannica*, set in India during the British Raj, one is getting an odd compromise between an old play and a new one.

But although indefensible in theory, in practice the free 'version' by a living playwright sometimes works; and, in the case of *Undiscovered Country*, triumphantly so since Schnitzler's play is itself a brilliant piece and Stoppard has not unduly imposed his own style on the text. Unlike some of his later versions of European classics, you wouldn't know it was by Stoppard unless the programme-credits told you so.

Schnitzler's play, written in 1911, is set in a country villa near Vienna and a hotel in the Dolomites and is about what one character calls 'this bogus civility between people made wretched by jealousy, cowardice, lust.' The surface is one of decorous politeness: underneath it lurks panic, death and an insane preoccupation with honour. The central character, Friedrich Hofreiter, is a manufacturer of incandescent light-bulbs who combines a hectic, exuberant public demeanour with a racked, tortured private self. He also seems to be surrounded by mortality and decay. We learn that a close friend of his plunged to his death while mountain-climbing; we hear that another friend of his, a Russian concert pianist, has committed suicide apparently because of his unrequited love for Hofreiter's wife; and the action climaxes in a duel between Hofreiter and a young naval lieutenant who has casually cuckolded him. Just as much as in *Rosencrantz and Guildenstern*, the smell of death pervades the whole atmosphere of the play.

What Stoppard's version (vivaciously directed by Peter Wood and remarkably played by John Wood as a Hofreiter alternating between champagne gaiety and fevered neurosis) achieved was a combination of leisured, bourgeois wit and a sense of the enigmatic uncertainty of human behaviour. 'Didn't he leave a note?' someone asks of the self-slaughtering Russian concert pianist. 'Korsakow wouldn't be seen dead with a suicide note,' came the swift reply. And when Dr Von Aigner, a lubricious hotelier, reports how he once climbed a dangerous mountain out of guilt and despair at the termination of his marriage, Hofreiter replies: 'Listen, if every erring husband started climbing up the nearest cliff . . . the Dolomites would afford a very strange spectacle.'

That same scene also reveals the reason why Stoppard was attracted to creating his own version of Schniztler: there is a strange consonance between their preoccupation with order, chaos and the need to beat back the darkness. Asked by Hofreiter why he parted from a wife he clearly adored, Von Aigner replies:

'Why I betrayed her? *You* ask *me*? Haven't you ever thought what a strange unchartered country is human behaviour? So many contradictions find room in us – love and deceit, . . . loyalty and betrayal . . . worshipping one woman, yet longing for another, or several others. We try to bring order into our lives as best we can; but that very order has something unnatural about it. The natural condition is chaos. Yes, Hofreiter, the soul . . . is an undiscovered country as the poet once said . . . though it could equally well have been the manager of a hotel.'

Freud, of course, was a contemporary and admirer of Schnitzler's

135

and it is fascinating to see how the conflict between Love and Death runs through the Austrian dramatist's work just as much as it does through Freudian casebooks.

You can see why Stoppard enjoyed working on this particular play. It deals with primordial themes in an exquisitely civilised setting. It keeps a very Stoppardian balance between the artificial and the real. It also, I suspect, allowed Stoppard to write about the vagaries of human passion through the perspective of another man's work. It coincided with his own gradual shift from the purely cerebral play of ideas to the exploration of real human dilemmas and permitted him to extend his emotional range while remaining faithful to Schnitzler's intentions.

Dogg's Hamlet, Cahoot's Macbeth

Not that life is ever that simple. At the same time as *Night and Day* was running at the Phoenix and *Undiscovered Country* at the Olivier (both plays deriving from mainstream European naturalism), Stoppard also had performed in London two linked one-act plays, *Dogg's Hamlet, Cahoot's Macbeth* that were anti-naturalistic in style and cerebral. They brought together several of Stoppard's prime concerns: Shakespeare, Wittgenstein, language-games, and the heavy-handed persecution of artists (and many others) in Czechoslovakia. *Dogg's Hamlet, Cahoot's Macbeth* were written for BARC: the British American Repertory Company which was devised by Ed Berman as a means of allowing non-star actors to function on either side of the Atlantic. It was a useful, if short-lived, idea. And it encouraged Stoppard to conceive an entertainment that was playful and serious at the same time, but, one is bound to say, nowhere near as successful as a naturalistic masterpiece like *Professional Foul* in plunging our noses into the Czech situation or achieving what Benedict Nightingale called a 'committed hilarity'.

Dogg's Hamlet (an extension of the earlier *Dogg's Our Pet*) was based partly on Wittgenstein's notion of language as an assemblage of games as various in their nature as hopscotch, polo and chess. Stoppard himself says, 'The appeal to me consisted in the possibility of writing a play which had to teach the audience the language the play was written in.' So we see a

136

group of schoolboys, with names like Able, Baker, Charlie, erecting a platform for a prize-giving and speaking a nonsense-lingo (Dogg) in which words often have the opposite meaning from their familiar associations. Thus when a schoolboy says to his headmaster 'Cretinous pig-faced git?' he is actually enquiring 'Have you got the time please, sir?' What complicates the situation is that the boys are also rehearsing the school play and lapse into Shakespearian English and that a lorry-driver, Easy, arrives with a load of blocks from Leamington Spa and also speaks received English. When he cries matily to the headmaster, 'Afternoon, Squire' he doesn't realise that translates in Dogg as 'Get stuffed, you bastard.' And when the headmaster says to him 'Moronic creep' his natural instinct is to grab him by the lapels not realising he is referring to the maroon carpet. Stoppard's point is perfectly clear: that language is an arbitrary means of signification. It also leads to some good jokes such as a figure of imperturbable regality beginning her speech to the assembled pupils with 'Scabs, slobs, yobs, yids, spicks, wops ...' But although Stoppard proves to his, and our, satisfaction that language is a form of game and that we can very quickly become attuned to the new rules (Easy soon becomes conversant with Dogg), one is secretly rather glad when the joke is over and the letters spelling out 'Dogg's Hamlet' appear on the assembled blocks.

After this slightly dogged opening what follows is, in theatrical terms, hilarious: a potted 15-minute version of *Hamlet* as performed by Stoppard's students to whom Shakespeare is clearly a foreign language. Stoppard is by no means the first person to appreciate both the laughs you can get and the shock effects you can create by chopping up Shakespeare and even transposing the lines. Many years ago in *Punch*, Paul Dehn came up with a potted *Macbeth* that boasted the memorable couplet, 'The devil damn thee black, thou cream-faced loon,/ Whom we invite to see us crowned at Scone.' And, on a marginally higher level, Charles Marowitz has offered his own collage versions of *Hamlet*, *Macbeth* and *Othello*.

Marowitz's collage-effects are, for me, less theatrical than Stoppard's collegiate humour which both makes the point that you can preserve the salient points of *Hamlet* in a boiled-down version and also says something about the modern world's impatient hunger for compression and its short-circuiting of human sensibility. First Stoppard brings on Shakespeare himself who, in an opening Prologue, confirms the opinion of the lady who said that *Hamlet* was full of quotations by offering us all the best-known lines ending with 'Cat will mew and Dogg will have his day'. We then launch into what Jack Kroll in *Newsweek* called 'transistorized Shakespeare'. No sooner, for instance, has Hamlet said 'To be or not to be that is the question' than Ophelia rushes in crying 'My lord' and is peremptorily told 'Get thee to a nunnery'. On stage, the effect is of watching Hamlet played at lightning speed by the Keystone Cops. The joke is not at the expense of Shakespeare but of a modern society that has little time for philosophical digressions or teased-out dilemmas, and craves incessant action executed by moral ciphers. Spurred to an encore, the cast then do a 90-second repeat of the whole play that leaves one helpless with laughter.

Cahoot's Macbeth, in the second half of the evening, also plays on the idea of truncated Shakespeare and the power of words to take on new meanings depending on the context in which they are used. The purpose here is anything but frivolous since it is to draw attention to the iniquities of the Czech regime and the fact that an acclaimed actor, Pavel Landovsky, (who was driving the car on the day in January, 1977 when police stopped him and his friend's car and seized the document that became known as Charter '77) had been driven from his profession in the theatre and obliged to take Living-Room Theatre into people's homes. Interestingly, there is a similar company in Britain that, on request, will come and perform *A Streetcar Named Desire* or *The Servant* in your home; but what for us is bourgeois titilation is in Czechoslovakia the only means of self-expression for outlawed actors.

Stoppard imagines such a troupe performing *Macbeth* in a private sitting-room with us, the theatre audience, becoming the assembled playgoers. The performance is then interrupted by a grotesque Inspector (a favourite Stoppard character) who is both more theatrical than the actors and a sinister-comic agent of repression. The play works on several levels: on one, it is a reminder of the horrific modern applicability of Shakespeare's tragedy with its theme of the illegal usurpation of power; on another, it is a jokey farce that uses (like *Rosencrantz and Guildenstern* and *The Real Inspector Hound*) the intrusion of reality into theatrical artifice.

It is a dangerous, tightrope-walking play because it makes us laugh at a situation that in real life is anything but funny. Stoppard gets away with it partly because of his own impeccable credentials as a human-rights campaigner, partly because there is nothing tentative or apologetic about his jokes, and partly because the laughs all point up the gravity of the situation. Discovering a telephone under a tea-cosy, the Inspector is perturbed:

> INSPECTOR: You've even got a telephone. I can see you're not at the bottom of the social heap. What do you do?
> HOSTESS: I'm an artist.
> INSPECTOR: Well it's not the first time I've been wrong.

In a country where, as Stoppard recorded in the *New York Review of Books*, you can find boilers stoked by economists, streets swept by men reading Henry James in English, where filing-clerks rise early to write articles for learned journals abroad and where third-rate time-servers are chauffeured around in black, bulbous Tatra 603s, the Inspector's response is all too apt. What Stoppard does in the play is depict the upside-down nature of a society in which a fine actor like Landovsky is acclaimed by the coarse-grained Inspector for his work as a factory floor-cleaner or a newspaper seller and in which language itself is corrupted. George Orwell in *1984* and *Animal Farm* reminded us that language and liberty are inter-twined and that when words are perverted or repressed so is freedom. Stoppard makes the same point through brutal, quick-fire comedy:

> INSPECTOR (*to* HOSTESS): Which one were you?
> HOSTESS: I'm not in it.
> INSPECTOR: You're in it, up to here. It's pretty clear to me that this flat is being used for entertaining men. There is a law about that you know.
> HOSTESS: I don't think Macbeth is what was meant.
> INSPECTOR: Who's to say what was meant? Words can be your friend or your enemy depending on who's throwing the book, so watch your language.

Maybe there is something too direct and up-front about the way Stoppard sends a figure like Orton's Inspector Truscott from *Loot* crashing around pointing out the way artists are degraded, rooms are bugged, language is twisted and Shakespeare becomes a reckless subversive in a police-state: the play lacks the subtlety of *Professional Foul*. But it gets its point across through a mixture of unashamed farce and clear statement; and never more so than when the Inspector points out that Shakespeare – Old Bill as he is known to the force – becomes all too contemporary in politically explosive situations:

> 'The fact is that when you get a universal and timeless writer like Shakespeare there's a strong feeling that he could be spitting in the eyes of the beholder when he should be keeping his mind on Verona – hanging around the "gents". You know what I mean. Unwittingly, of course. He didn't know what he was doing, at least you couldn't prove he did, which is what makes the chief so prejudiced against him.'

I am reminded of Ian McKellen's account in the book, *A Night at the Theatre*, of playing Richard II in Bratislava in 1969 after the Russian invasion of Czechoslovakia. During the scene where Richard weeps for joy to stand upon his kingdom once again, as McKellen spoke the familiar lines, 'Dear earth, I do salute thee with my hand' he became aware of a collective mewing, grieving, crying sound from the audience: a token of their recognition of the earth as their only symbol of a future freedom and a continuing past. Stoppard also never lets us forget the relevance of *Macbeth* to modern Czechoslovakia even to the point of having a police-siren wail as Macduff cries 'Bleed, bleed, poor country.'

The good thing about *Cahoot's Macbeth* is that it brings home to spectators in privileged Britain and America a glimmer of what it must be like to live in a country where the simple act of putting on a play may land you in gaol. It is affirmative, committed, political: all those things one has always wished Stoppard to be. My only real cavil is that Stoppard's love of diagrammatic neatness slightly runs away with him and he rounds off the play by bringing back the Dogg-speaking lorry-driver, Easy, with a load of timber for Birnam Wood, the actors tune in to Dogg themselves and deliver the final speeches of *Macbeth* in this alternative language. It's a clever way of bringing the evening full circle and of harnessing Stoppard's fascination with word-games and Shakespeare to the uncontainability of the Czech situation as Malcolm takes the crown off Macbeth's head and places it on his own. The implication is that change is inevitable. But, lively as *Dogg's Hamlet, Cahoot's Macbeth* is, you feel at the end of the evening you haven't quite seen Stoppard stretching his talent to his fullest; and that his true direction for the future lies away from theatre-as-game and towards the excavation of true feeling. It wouldn't be fair to say that this generously-donated double-bill shows Stoppard BARC-ing up the wrong tree but it seems a digression from his exploration of a refined and heightened naturalism.

On The Razzle

Stoppard kept us waiting a bit longer for his next adventure in realism. In 1980 he was represented only by a script for an ill-fated film version of Graham Greene's *The Human Factor* which was under-funded and lugubriously directed by an ailing Otto Preminger: the result, honestly undertaken, reportedly reduced Stoppard to tears. Then, on September 22, 1981 at the Lyttelton, Stoppard came up with a very free adaptation of an 1842 comedy by the Austrian actor-manager, Johann Nestroy, *Einen Jux will er sich machen*, here entitled *On The Razzle*. Verbally, it is Stoppard's most joke-packed play: the text is a dense web of puns, Spoonerisms, innuendos, conceits, tricks that produce a steady chuckle of delight. But although the play is very funny, Stoppard sacrifices the danger and momentum of farce on the altar of verbal richness. Loading every rift with ore, he slows the action down; and the result is an engaging romp rather than something with the single-directional energy of classic farce. Stoppard, I suspect, is too clever, too much in love with verbal decoration to be a great farce-writer.

On The Razzle has a lineage as complex as that of a Yorkist monarch in *The Wars of the Roses*. Back in 1835, John Oxenford, a lawyer, translator and for many years a drama critic of *The Times*, wrote a one-act farce, *A Day Well Spent*, which was a hit at the Lyceum. In 1842, Johann Nepomuk Nestroy turned this into a social comedy, employing a variety of

Viennese dialects, called *Einen Jux will er sich machen* (He's Out For A Fling). It's a whirl of confusion about three groups of people all spending a traumatic night on the town. Zangler, an elderly small town grocer, heads to the wicked city both for the Grocers' Company parade and to further his marriage plans to a Viennese milliner. He leaves two assistants minding the store: his chief clerk Weinberl (now promoted partner) and Christopher (promoted from apprentice to clerk) but they, too, head to Vienna for a fling before the cares of responsibility weigh them down. Zangler's niece and ward, Marie, is also despatched to his Viennese sister-in-law to keep her out of the clutches of her impoverished admirer, Sonders.

Inevitably all their paths converge: first of all, at a fashionable restaurant where Weinberl and Christopher are entertaining Zangler's fiancée and her best friend behind a screen, and where Zangler is on the look-out for the fugitive Marie and Sonders; and then again, at the sister-in-law's flat, where almost everyone turns up under false identities. Zangler's assistants make their getaway in the nick of time and, back at the shop next morning, they return fractionally before their suspicious master. As in traditional comedy, everyone is neatly paired off. Zangler is to marry his milliner. Weinberl, his new partner, will take to wife her best friend. And Sonders has inherited a small fortune so he can have Marie.

The idea of two assistants turning the tables on their boss and having a youthful fling seems to have a mythic attraction. Thornton Wilder took up the story in *The Merchant of Yonkers* (1938) and a post-war modification of it – *The Matchmaker* (1954). His main addition was the character of the rampageous matchmaker, Dolly Levi, and his main subtraction the removal of a sub-plot in which the two adventurers return from the city in time to prevent their employer being burgled. Then, in 1963, came the Broadway musical *Hello Dolly*, of which the high point was the arrival of Dolly Levi at the Harmonia Gardens Restaurant where the waiters greet her as if she were a combination of Cleopatra, the Queen of Sheba and John D. Rockefeller. Finally – for the present – came Stoppard with his version going back to the Nestroy structure and relocating the action in Vienna, but making it a Vienna mad on all things Scottish. Stoppard builds up the part of a rantipole Coachman, adds a little ragamuffin for Christopher to boss around and includes, in the words of Peter Branscombe in the *Times Literary Supplement*, 'sexual and lavatorial jokes of a vigour and raciness unthinkable in Metternich's Vienna'.

Stoppard, working from a literal translation by Neville and Stephen Plaice, makes no pretence that his version is anything other than a free adaptation. Writing in the National Theatre programme, he says: 'I'm not really a believer in the hypothesis of true translation. The particularity of a writer's voice is a mysterious collusion of sound and sense. The certain knowledge that a translation will miss it by at least an inch makes it less dreadful to miss it by a yard.' One wonders how he might react to free foreign versions of his own work that made no attempt to reproduce his rhythms, cadences or distinctive tone of voice. But the problems posed by *On The Razzle* are less ethical than practical; and the central one is whether you can combine the drive and desperation of farce with densely-textured verbal comedy. The essence of farce, as Eric Bentley pointed out in *The Life of the Drama*, is outrage to family piety, desecration of the household gods, the fulfilment by violently active human beings of our most treasured, unmentionable wishes. You don't get much of that in *On The Razzle*. You get confusion, the chase, a tissue of mistaken identities. But, judged purely as farce, the piece doesn't quite work because nothing vital seems at stake (What will happen to Weinberl and Christopher if they are discovered? At the least, social embarrassment: at the worst, the sack.), no one is reduced to a state of flustered desperation and the piece is so encrusted with jokes that it can never achieve the headlong, spinning pace that farce requires. Stoppard loves farce, but, as a writer, he lacks the simplicity and ingenousness that makes it possible.

The best way to take *On The Razzle* is as a pot-pourri of jokes with allusions to the Marx Brothers, S.J. Perelman, Eddie Braben, John Cleese, Danny Kaye, Bud Flanagan and a host of others. In some ways, it reads better than it plays since on the page you have time to pick up the verbal cross-hatching and spot the 57 varieties of jokes being used. Though sometimes the web of allusions sinks into self-indulgence:

SONDERS: Then I'll stay here and marry her, if that's your wont.
ZANGLER: And meanwhile in Brussels your inheritance

will be eaten by codicils letting my wont wait upon her like the poor cat with the haddock.

There seems no good reason why a self-important Austrian grocer should be misquoting Shakespeare or speaking in complex puns that fly past almost unnoticed in the theatre. Indeed what is striking is how everyone in the play talks like a chip off the old Stoppard. Consider Weinberl on the hazards of the grocery trade:

'We sit here idly twisting paper into cones, flicking a duster over piles of preserved figs and pyramids of uncertain dates, swatting flies like wanton gods off the north face of the Emmental, and gazing into the street.'

The cleverness is undeniable. But again you are left wondering why a grocer's assistant – whose very innocence and unworldliness is the motivating force of the plot – should be sitting around uttering perfectly-chiselled phrases and making wry, scholarly allusions to *King Lear*.

Where Stoppard does score is in quick, agile repartee, particularly when it is laced with sexual inuendo and springs from character. Thus:

ZANGLER: Marie is very vulnerable. If she so much as sets foot outside the door she's going to catch it from me.
MELCHIOR: How long have you had it?

And again:

MARIE: Oh, August, you're a terrible man, kiss me again. You made me feel all funny down there.
SONDERS: Oh Marie
MARIE: I mean in the cellar.

And again (referring to Sonders and Marie):

ZANGLER: They're at a table in the garden. Let me know if he gets up.
MELCHIOR: I'll throw a bucket of water over them.

This is based on a very English tradition of humour in which all

144

conversation is mined for its hidden sexual references and in which the simplest pronoun or preposition – 'it' and 'up' in this case – takes on connotations of naughtiness. Morecambe and Wise refined this kind of thing into an art so that language became a minefield of sexual allusions and it is rather refreshing to find the highly sophisticated Stoppard has inherited this schoolboy sense of humour: a dirty mind is a joy forever.

Purists might object – indeed did object – that this has nothing to do with Nestroy and that Stoppard is here wasting the precious resource of his wit. And it is true that one misses in *On The Razzle* the precisely-rooted social comedy of the original, and the mixture of pathos and frenzy in the idea of two young men rushing to the city to acquire memories and a past before they settle down to years of dreary respectability in the grocery-trade. At the National Theatre Carl Tom's grocery-shop – with its chutes and canisters, cages and counters – was such a beautiful piece of design one wondered why Weinberl and Christopher ever wanted to leave it. But, although it is not a perfect farce and the pudding is over-egged, it would be churlish to deny that *On The Razzle* makes me laugh a lot. Laughter seems to me its own justification; and, as I think back to the spectacle of Harold Innocent as the lubricious, burly coachman crying, 'I have the finest pair of chestnuts of any coachman in the city', I find it easy to forgive Stoppard his verbal trespasses.

The Real Thing

Two charges have been persistently levelled at Stoppard over the years: one is that his writing betrays no visible commitment to a cause: the other is that he fights shy of the basic human emotions. *Every Good Boy Deserves Favour* and *Professional Foul* answer the first charge through their total commitment to human rights. *The Real Thing*, written for the commercial manager Michael Codron and first mounted at the Strand Theatre in November, 1982, proves that Stoppard can write about the pain of adultery and the excitement of love without sacrificing one iota of his wit and intelligence. This is his most mature play, his best-structured play, indeed his best-written play in that the speeches spring off the page and stage and nothing is wasted. Mike Nichols's New York production proved something else about Stoppard, that the skilled artifice of Peter

Wood's London productions is only one vision of him as a writer. There may be others. His plays can be played with a much greater degree of emotional reality.

What actually is *The Real Thing* about? A whole host of matters. To what can we commit ourselves publicly and privately? What, in fact, is the real thing in love, writing, politics? Is love unliterary? Do we inherit our notions of 'good writing' from what the good writers tell us? Is any public engagement with a cause the result of private disturbance? Is one man's Procul Harum another man's Verdi? Do concepts like politics, justice, patriotism have any existence outside our perception of them? Is adultery possible without pain? The play's structure, like a series of Chinese boxes one deftly tucked inside another, is a direct reflection of its thematic pre-occupation with the real thing. But what makes this play unusual for Stoppard is that it is not merely written with panache (we expect that) but that it is also moving and painful.

It is fascinating that many of Stoppard's contemporaries have, in recent years, written ingeniously structured plays about the same theme of adultery. Harold Pinter's *Betrayal* charted the politics of infidelity and struck an unusual note by moving backwards in time rather than forwards: the result was drily intelligent. Peter Nichols's *Passion Play* tackled middle-aged infidelity by constructing alter egos for the central husband-and-wife characters which both helped to reveal their innermost thoughts and to intensify the theme of suffering hinted at in the equivocal title. But if I had to pin down the difference between Stoppard's play and these, it would be that *The Real Thing* branches out from the subject of adultery to take on board so many other issues, and to raise so many questions about the values by which we live. I question some of Stoppard's conclusions without doubting for a moment that this is one of the finest British plays since the war.

To appreciate its intricacy fully one needs to look in some detail at its eleven scenes and the way in which Stoppard allows ideas to echo, reverberate and expand. Always, however, one needs to remember that the key question is 'What is the real thing?' That point is posed in the first scene when we watch Max and Charlotte, two smart, clever people saying smart, clever things. Max is an architect who is seen constructing a pyramidical house of cards as his wife returns home apparently

146

from a business-trip to Geneva for Sotheby's. Behind the bantering dialogue ('How's old Geneva then? Franc doing well? – Who? – The Swiss franc. Is it doing well?') we realise that Max has discovered his wife has left her passport behind and has apparently been unfaithful. He reacts with cool, witty derision and the scene ends with his taking a miniature Alp in a glass-bowl out of her airport bag and creating a snowstorm-effect which envelops the whole stage.

This is the kind of thing we expect from Stoppard: verbally stylish reactions to emotional events and a high theatricality. Only at the start of the next scene do we realise that this is a scene from a play, *House of Cards*, written by the protagonist of *The Real Thing*, Henry. It is worth noting that in Peter Wood's London production this opening scene was played with much the same cool artifice as the rest of the evening. In Mike Nichols's Broadway version the whole scene was played in heavily inverted commas and with a heightened Cowardesque camp so that even the slowest member of the audience would realise he was watching a play-within-a-play. This last decision was right because what Stoppard is doing here is staking out the territory he will explore in the rest of the play: the way one reacts to a partner's assumed infidelity, the conflict between elegant expression and impassioned commitment: (Max: 'I'm showing an interest in your work. I thought you liked me showing an interest in your work. *My* showing. Save the gerund and screw the whale.'); the suspicion that leads one partner to ransack another's belongings while they are away. But what Stoppard is concerned with, above all, in this scene is showing the unreality of conventional stage adultery. 'Sincerity in society,' Somerset Maugham once wrote, 'is like an iron girder in a house of cards.' What Stoppard goes on to show is that life is neither as tidy nor as elegant as Henry makes it; and that when the iron girder of sincerity is introduced the house of cards naturally collapses.

The second scene, in Henry's home the next morning, both exposes the theatrical artificiality of the first and extends and develops the whole argument about the real thing. We learn that Charlotte, the actress of the first scene, is Henry's wife and that Max, the actor of the first scene, is being cuckolded by Henry. In narrow plot terms, the chief function of this scene is to reveal that Henry is having an affair with Max's wife Annie. But Stoppard also raises the whole question as to whether there is a measurable 'real thing' in music: whether there is, in fact, an absolute standard of definable excellence or whether everything depends on the arbitrariness of individual taste. He does this through Henry's problem in choosing his eight records for *Desert Island Discs* (many Americans I spoke to doubted the real existence of such a programme), and through the fact he gets a bigger kick out of the Righteous Brothers' version of 'You've Lost That Lovin' Feeling' than ever he did out of hearing Callas at Covent Garden. Who is to say he is wrong? If a work of popular art makes a greater impact on an individual than an acknowleged classic, does that not mean it is just as good? It's the kind of problem critics confront daily: I recall Harold Hobson once writing that Brendan Behan's *The Hostage* may not be a masterpiece but that it had the impact of a masterpiece on him.

Stoppard also raises in this crucial scene the whole question of political commitment. Is it ever pure and disinterested? Or is Henry right when he says, 'Public postures have the configuration of private derangement.' All the evidence Stoppard adduces suggests the latter. Annie is on the Justice for Brodie Committee: an organisation for the defence of a private soldier who has gone to prison for committing an act of arson at the Cenotaph as a protest against Cruise missiles. Henry gets Annie to tell the story of how she met Brodie on a train and pours ironic scorn both on the campaign for Brodie and on the language of protest ('he got hammered by an emotional backlash'). But we learn at the end of the scene that Henry's reactionary posture and needling provocation was 'just so I could look at you without it looking funny'. Furthermore we learn that Max and Annie are vehemently opposed to nuclear missiles largely because they own a cottage near the camp, that Max puts a squash game before a meeting of the Brodie Committee (there is some confusion as to whether this took place before the lunch drinks or is scheduled for later) and that Annie puts her love for Henry before her commitment to Brodie ('Let him rot.'). I happen to think Stoppard is wrong: that there is such a thing as scrupulously-motivated political protest. I do not believe that those who campaign against Cruise missiles, Apartheid or (in Stoppard's case) the suppression of human rights in Eastern Europe are motivated by 'private derangement'. But it's a point of view and it is pushed through with logical consistency.

Before one appropriates all Henry's opinions as Stoppard's, it is worth pointing out that the play (and this scene) offers a considered criticism of Henry. He is told in this scene that the women in his plays are victims of his fantasy, that people in real life don't behave as they do in his plays, that he pushes domestic banalities to one side, and that he may have all the answers but 'having all the answers is not what life's all about'. Stoppard admitted in a 1984 *New York Times* interview with Mel Gussow that the play is 'self-referential'. I would say it is extremely self-critical. Stoppard has put a lot of himself into Henry and turned the play into something of a self-indictment.

The cunning of the play's structure (and its obsession with the 'real thing' in love and politics) becomes apparent in the third scene. Stoppard himself told *Time* magazine that one of the challenges he set himself was 'to structure a play by repeating a given situation – a man in a room with his wife showing up – three times each differently.' He does this in Scene 1, Scene 3 and Scene 10; and there are both echoes between the scenes and fascinating discords.

In Scene 1 Max (the actor) discovers his stage-wife's supposed adultery through a piece of circumstantial evidence: a passport. In Scene 3, Max (the person) discovers his real wife's actual adultery through circumstantial evidence: Henry's blood-spotted handkerchief. This time there is no smart repartee. Max cries 'You're filthy. You filthy cow. You rotten filthy-', kicks the radio (ironically playing 'You've Lost That Lovin' Feeling' from Henry's *Desert Island Discs* programme) and flings himself on Annie in a mixture of assault and embrace. It is, in one sense, artificial (radios are rarely playing such appropriate music at emotional turning-points) but, in another, it is much closer to the twisted, tortured, love-hate reactions people have at such moments.

Stoppard doesn't just use verbal and thematic echoes to link scenes: he also uses visual parallels. Scene 4 between Henry and Annie, now shacked up together, echoes Scene 2 between Henry and Charlotte in its arrangement of door and furniture. But where Scene 2 showed the waspishness of an ailing relationship, this one deals with the exploratory gaiety of a burgeoning one. Where Henry before had people in on a Sunday he now rejoices in 'the insularity of passion'. This scene also introduces another theme: how do you write love? Can you even express 'the real thing'. Henry is trying to write a play for Annie (he never seems

149

to complete it) but finds 'I don't know how to write love. I try to write it properly and it just comes out embarrassing. It's either childish or it's rude.' Annie, however, is rehearsing *Miss Julie* and runs through a scene with Henry which makes several points. One is that lust (if not love) can be expressed indirectly through sub-text. Another is that passion transcends class and that there is, in Strindberg's play, a magnetic attraction between the falling lady and the upwardly-mobile valet: a hint of the Annie-Brodie, Annie-Billy relationships yet to come. This play is a dense tissue of internal cross-references (Switzerland, where Charlotte went in the first scene and where Henry wrote his Jean-Paul Sartre play while listening to The Crystals, crops up yet again in the *Miss Julie* extract). The miracle of *The Real Thing* is that the endless whispering-gallery echoes are combined with an individual life and freshness in each scene. This scene has just the right teasing tension of two people both very much in love and both very professionally preoccupied. And when, at the end of it, Annie goes through Henry's papers it is both a reminder of the way partners invade each other's belongings and a totally natural, spontaneous gesture. That is real craft.

In the past, Stoppard's verbal dexterity has sometimes camouflaged an emotional stasis: most notably in *Travesties*. Here, writing in a style of heightened naturalism, he constantly carries the drama forward developing and extending his ideas with symphonic skill. Act Two starts with Scene 5 and is set two years later. Without a word being spoken, we see that Henry has been transformed by love: he is now listening to Verdi on the record-player and apparently enjoying it. The crux of this scene is a debate on what 'the real thing' is in writing. Is it simply setting down one's experience? Or is it having the craft, skill or plain knack of making words come alive on the page? Annie wants to do a TV play by Brodie, about his victimisation by the authorities, in order to draw attention to his plight and get his sentence reduced. Henry objects that Brodie can't write: Annie counters that the rules of good writing are simply laid down by precedence and other writers.

It is a fascinating art versus truth debate. If Annie were less scornful of the Eng. Lit. Brigade she might have brought in on her side Wordsworth's preface to the 1800 edition of the *Lyrical Ballads* where he talks of poetry as 'the spontaneous overflow of powerful feelings' and where he describes the poet as 'a man speaking to men'. But, in fact, she is outgunned by Henry who, in a now famous speech, picks up a cricket bat and explains how with the deftest flick of the wrist it can send a ball travelling 200 yards in 4 seconds: good writing should have the same deftness and ease. This speech contains more passion and feeling than anything in Stoppard to date and is suffused with lyrical pleasure. Annie counters by asking Henry to re-write Brodie's play. Henry's response is to attack the naïveté of Brodie's view of the world and he does so in a manner that both seems to speak for Stoppard and to raise the whole question as to the nature of reality :

'There is, I suppose, a world of objects which have a certain form, like this coffee mug. I turn it, and it has no handle. I tilt it, and it has no cavity. But there is something real here which is always a mug with a handle, I suppose. But politics, justice, patriotism – they aren't even like coffee mugs. There's nothing real there separate from our perception of them. So if you try to stick labels on them, 'farce', 'fraud', 'condemned', and try to change them as though there were something there to change, you'll get frustrated and frustration will finally make you violent. If you know this and proceed with humility, you may perhaps alter people's perceptions so that they behave a little differently at that axis of behaviour where we locate politics or justice; but if you don't know this, then you're acting on a mistake. Prejudice is the expression of this mistake.'

This is a classic statement of the Stoppardian position: the relativity of perception, the subjectivity in our use of key words, the danger of totally inflexible absolutes. Stoppard suggests the writer may change people's outlook rather than events. What this misses out, however, is the *saeva indignatio* that lies at the heart of much good writing. If writers down the ages had taken this line, it is hard to believe we would ever have had Aristophanes' *Lysistrata*, Shakespeare's *Troilus and Cressida*, Milton's *Areopagitica*, Ben Jonson's *Volpone*, Swift's *Gulliver's Travels*, Dostoyevsky's *The Possessed*. It also overlooks a point made in *Professional Foul* that there is a consensus about the meaning of certain words like 'justice' and 'freedom' on which civilised, democratic societies act and which they enshrine in

Declarations of Rights. Stoppard himself has acted on the belief that 'justice' has been denied or besmirched in the Eastern bloc countries; and that is not just his perception of the matter. But this is a play not a pamphlet and the key point is that Stoppard is once again asking us to consider what 'the real thing' is in matters of art, life and politics.

It is a play that also works through action and reaction. Scene 6 set on a train (the setting for Annie's reported first encounter with Brodie) introduces a new character in Billy with whom Annie is due to appear in a Glasgow production of *'Tis Pity She's a Whore*. Annie tries to justify the fact she is travelling first class by applying Henry's arguments to the class-system ('There's nothing really *there* – it's just the way you see it. Your perception.') and is quite rightly attacked by Billy for her glibness. Conversely, Henry's proposition that 'Public postures have the configuration of private derangements' is given a boost by Billy who says that he will do Brodie's TV play if Annie does it. The interlocking ironies are also extended when Billy starts to declare his 'real' passion for Annie through the 'unreal' medium of a scene from Ford's play which deals with a guilty, furtive and incestuous relationship. In Peter Wood's London production this scene was part of the overall, artificial framework: in Mike Nichols's more naturalistic Broadway version the railway-carriage appeared before us with magical speed leaving us to relate the scene to what had gone before.

Scene 7 echoes Scene 2 in that it places Henry and Charlotte back in their old living-room. The acerbity of mis-matched partners has been replaced by the easy tolerance of the separated. On one level, the scene adds to the Chinese-box nature of the play in that Charlotte has been living with an architect ('I call him the architect of my misfortune') which was the profession of the fictive character played by Max at the start of the proceedings.

But, more crucially, the scene reminds us that the play is very much about the sentimental education of Henry and the flaws in his attitude to love. Henry discovers that Charlotte had nine lovers in the course of their marriage and says, rather defeatedly, that he thought they had made a commitment. 'There are no commitments,' says the hard-headed Charlotte, 'only bargains. And they have to be made again every day. You think making a commitment is *it*. Finish. You think it sets like a concrete platform and it'll take any strain you want to put on it. You're committed. You don't have to prove anything.' Charlotte ends the scene by warning him against the heedless romanticism that assumes relationships are infinitely durable; and the point is swiftly underlined by the short scene 8 in which Annie and Billy are rehearsing *'Tis Pity* and he, in character of Giovanni, gets under her defences and overcomes her guilt.

Scene 9 introduces Henry's daughter Debbie, whom he goes to see in her squat, and further defines contrasting attitudes to love. I am reminded of a not dissimilar scene in John Osborne's *Inadmissible Evidence* where Maitland, the disintegrating solicitor, encounters his teenage daughter and – in a scene of pain and tenderness – offloads many of his prejudices against the young. Stoppard, to his credit, shows there is something to be said for Debbie's realistic and shrewd acceptance of ephemeral sexual relationships as against Henry's romantic belief in the importance of 'knowing and being known'. But the bruising irony of this well-written scene comes when Henry asks Debbie if she liked his last play:

DEBBIE: What – *House of Cards*? Well, it wasn't about anything, except did she have it off or didn't she? What a crisis. Infidelity amongst the architect-class. Again.
HENRY: It was about self-knowledge through pain.
DEBBIE: No, it was about did she have it off or didn't she?
HENRY: A discerning minority appreciated the irony of his false accusation pushing her into making it true.

What is true of *House of Cards* turns out to be true of *The Real Thing*. On the surface, it may look like another of those well-heeled adultery plays. But Henry also gains self-knowledge through pain (rather more intensely than Max appeared to do in the play-within-the-play). Henry also makes a false accusation to Annie that also propels her towards a real affair. Again, the scene multiplies the ironies while making its own statement about the gulf between youth and age.

Scene 10 is the third of Stoppard's carefully-placed episodes showing a man in a room awaiting his wife's return. Like Scenes 1 and 3, it starts with a man alone filling in time. Like those it also contains accusations of adultery based on circumstantial evidence: in this case Henry's phone-call to Glasgow which tells him that his wife caught the sleeper while she claims to have come down on the early-morning train. Like Scene 1, it also tells us the husband has ransacked his wife's things in desperation. But the real point of the scene is that the once-cool, smugly unjealous Henry is now reduced to emotional chaos and the once subjugated Annie has even started to correct his grammar. Nothing is set in concrete; relationships change.

> HENRY: Yes, you'd behave better than me. . . . I don't believe in behaving well. I don't believe in debonair relationships. 'How's your lover today, Amanda?' 'In the pink, Charles. How's yours?' I believe in mess, tears, pain, self-abasement, loss of self-respect, nakedness. Not caring doesn't seem much different from not loving. Did you?

This is what Debbie would call a did-she-have-it-off-or-didn't-she scene with the crucial difference that it is filled with the emotional rawness and jagged suspicion one finds in life itself.

Scene 11 is short: the TV version of Brodie's play. Annie sits reading on the train (as she did at the start of Scene 6) and Billy accosts her with 'Excuse me, is this seat taken?' But we are back with the question of what 'the real thing' is. This is Annie's initial meeting with Brodie now played by Billy and re-written by Henry: it is now at least two removes from life itself and, as we listen to Henry's dialogue, we note that it is technically better than Brodie's but has lost the lumpen authenticity of its original author's. A play, good or bad, has to be an expression of its author's personality.

By now the play's movement has begun to focus on Henry's despair and the gulf between his attempt at dignified cuckoldry and his aching, total need for Annie's love. Scene 12 starts with him once again listening to the radio (music is vital in this play). He has now moved from The Crystals and the Ronettes to Bach's Air on a G String – which he ironically claims is a lift from Procul Harum. But the point is he is attempting to be something which he is not: rational, unaffected, debonair as he lets Annie take a phone-call from Billy on her way to rehearse *Three Sisters* (another play about adultery, would-be dignified cuckoldry and emotional despair). Annie is now clearly having an affair. 'Tell me to stop and I'll stop,' she says. 'I can't,' says Henry. I'd just be the person who stopped you.' But the most moving moment in all Stoppard comes at the end of the scene when Annie departs and Henry, who has behaved impeccably throughout, puts on a record of Procul Harum, listens to it and smiles and then utters a heartrending cry of 'Oh, please, please, please, please *don't.*' This seems not just like a vital moment in Henry's sentimental education but in Stoppard's also in its recognition of downright pain.

Scene 13 ties all the threads of the play together and leaves us with something rare in modern drama: an optimistic conclusion. We at last meet the real Brodie who turns out to be graceless, thuggish and anything but a working-class hero. If the play has been asking what 'the real thing' is in art, politics, love we get some hints at possible answers in this scene. Henry has re-written Brodie's play for the box but the result is not 'the real thing' artistically and has not even been the cause of Brodie's release from gaol: he's out because the missiles he was marching against require money that would have been used on the prison system. That's a bit glib since government spending does not work in that way; but it nudges home the point that art is rarely socially useful and also that you cannot, in art, fake an indignation you don't feel. On the political front, we learn that Private Brodie's desecration at the Cenotaph was inspired not by moral fervour but by infatuation with Annie which confirms Henry's original point about privately-motivated public postures. But, on the emotional score, Henry has learned that 'the real thing' is not an idealised, devouring, exclusive, colonizing love but one that admits the other person's flawed individuality. As Henry turns up 'I'm a Believer' on the radio he seems to have come close to the real thing in at least one department.

Rich as the play is, there are arguments in it I would question. I believe Stoppard sets up a false, too easy antithesis between the guileful, apolitical craftsman–writer and the prejudiced, primitive playwright who uses words like blunt instruments. Ironic eloquence and impassioned views are not incompatible; and one finds in the work of David Hare, Howard Brenton, Trevor Griffiths, to name but three, strong convictions and a flexible style. Examined closely the notion that 'public postures have the configuration of private derangements' is insupportable. As Benedict Nightingale superbly wrote: 'Am I deranged when I wonder if it's morally acceptable to aim H-bombs at Moscow? Is Tom merely sublimating childhood feelings of rejection when he writes indignant plays about the abuse of human rights in his native Czechoslovakia and elsewhere? Must we dismiss the campaigns of, say, Wilberforce, Silverman and Sakharov as emotionally dishonest "postures"?' I don't think one need press the point further.

The virtues of *The Real Thing* easily outweigh its vices. It combines structural intricacy with profound feeling, a middle-class adultery comedy with an examination of art, language, politics, philosophy even. This time Stoppard has made a Fabergé egg but one that contains meat and substance and I surmise the play will be one of the handful written since the war that may be performed in the next century when manners and *mores* have changed. Watching Jeremy Irons and Glenn Close in the New York production, I also realised how much naturalistic detail Stoppard can take. In Mr Irons there was a wonderful mixture of emotional hesitancy (he blushed and looked nervously away when Annie cried 'Touch me' in the second scene) and fierce longing: in Ms Close there was warmth, ardour, sexual vibrancy. All the naturalistic details were there down to the latest copy of a theatrical magazine that Max brought with him to the Sunday brunch. Stoppard's play can take this because it is grounded in truth while flying high in its language and ideas. It shows him progressing as an artist and – conceivably – as a human being; and, in the words of Richard Corliss, in *Time*, 'it is the best cricket bat anyone has written in years'.

The Dog It Was That Died

Stoppard showed us the tragic side of espionage in his 1968 TV play, *Neutral Ground*. He deals with its comic aspects in his deliciously absurd radio play, *The Dog It Was That Died* (first broadcast on Radio 3 on December 9, 1982) which is the story of a spy and counter-spy being used by both the British and the Russians to the point that he cannot remember where his original loyalties lie. The play has, of course, a serious point: that the mechanics of espionage have a self-cancelling futility and that both East and West are locked in a pointlessly intricate game. This is not to say that Stoppard doesn't believe in the innate superiority of Western values: merely that when people are asked to articulate the ideological beliefs they are fighting for they lapse into terminal cliché. He goes further and suggests that the special glory of the English character lies in its freedom from dogma and theory and resides in a totally unself-conscious eccentricity. It could be objected that Stoppard's examples of dotty Englishness all come from the upper-income, clubman bracket; but the play, under all its le Carré-parody and Stephen Potterish quirkiness, is one of Stoppard's most sincere tributes to the amazing character of his adopted nation.

In form, the play does in radio terms what Stoppard did in the novel in *Lord Malquist and Mr Moon*, in television in *After Magritte* and in theatre in *Jumpers*. That is to say it starts with a chain of bizarre, illogical circumstances and then shows they have a perfectly rational explanation. Purvis, a double, triple and even quadruple agent working for a British secret-service agency known as Q6, throws himself off Chelsea Bridge. Before he does so, he posts a letter to his boss, Blair, setting down some odd facts: that the Q6 Chief has an opium den in Eaton Square; that he himself was looking forward to taking a belly-dancer to Buckingham Palace; that he is donating to Blair an heirloom that once belonged to a one-legged sea-captain who inspired Long John Silver; that he has left some money for a plaque on the wall of St Luke's where he was churchwarden, despite the fact that he was involved in a savoury incident there much disputed by the choirboys. Purvis's suicide is aborted by the fact that he lands on a dog lying on the deck of a barge that happened to be passing under Chelsea Bridge at high tide. But Stoppard keeps us listening partly to find out what on earth the meaning of Purvis's letter is.

To be truthful, not all the explanations are as ingenious as one might hope. Hogbin, another of Stoppard's dogged policemen, sets out with Blair to uncover the facts. The most startling turns out to be that the savoury business with choirboys involves an incident at St Luke's where Purvis cut a wedge out of the cheese-fancying vicar's vintage *Epoisses* and toasted it to make Welsh rarebit: Purvis blamed the choir but he was clearly the cheese-snitcher; the belly-dancer turns out to be Purvis's live-in companion whom he hoped to escort to a Buck House garden-party; the family heirloom was a parrot which Purvis intended to donate to Blair's own private Gothic folly, and the Chief does indeed smoke the odd opium-pipe in his den in Eaton Square.

The play is less about the deceptiveness of appearances than about the futility of espionage and the craziness of the English. The two aspects of the play come together when Blair visits Purvis in hospital and poor Purvis tries to work out the ideological basis of his confused career. When he quizzed the Russians about the ideological nub of the matter, they came up with 'historical inevitability'. But, as Purvis points out, the mere fact that something may be inevitable doesn't make it good so he made an excuse and left. Blair is even vaguer when asked about the rationale behind Western espionage:

PURVIS: . . . Can you remind me, what was the gist of it – the moral and intellectual foundation of Western society in a nutshell.

BLAIR: I'm sorry, my mind's gone blank.

PURVIS: Come on – democracy. . . . free elections, free expression, free market forces.

BLAIR: Oh yes, that was it.

PURVIS: Yes, but how did we deal with the argument that all this freedom merely benefits the people who already have the edge? I mean freedom of expression advantages the articulate. . . . Do you see?

BLAIR: You're going a bit fast for me, Purvis. I never really got beyond us being British and them being atheists and Communists.

Stoppard is doing two things here: sending up the espionage-world where people are so engrossed in tactics that they have quite forgotten what they are supposed to be defending but also delighting in that strange English reluctance to deal in theories and ideas. A lot of earlier Stoppard heroes believed that, if you studied the history of the world, you could find a pattern that would explain everything. Now Stoppard seems to be accepting the woolly day-to-day pragmatism that is part of English life.

In fact, if the play has a larger point it is that what we are fighting to defend is the right to pursue our eccentrically individual way of life. Blair, for instance, spends most of his time collecting clocks and constructing a crazy folly while his wife – apparently having an affair with his Chief – runs a donkey sanctuary. Purvis is sent to a rest-home on the Norfolk coast for cracked-up agents where the doctor is indistinguishable from the patients: one is a naval officer who talks entirely in extravagant nautical metaphors, another is a woman who dresses up as a matron to oblige a chap she got mixed up with in Washington; and even the doctor, who used to work in code-making consonantal transposition, ('Posetransing stantocons, titeg?') invites Blair to see the bats in his belfry. This thread of eccentric selfhood runs right through the play from Purvis's co-habitation with a Turkish belly-dancer, to the vicar who holds up matins for ten minutes to hunt for a missing piece of brick-red, Dijon-based *Epoisses*, and to the Chief who discusses such vital matters as which department shall pay for the dead dog over a bubbling opium-pipe. I have often noticed that people not born in England have an exaggerated regard for what they see as the oddities and peculiarities of the island race; and, though Stoppard came to live in England at the age of nine, he still sometimes seems to view the country with the detached amusement of an outsider.

The play also shows Stoppard's delight in radio itself: he uses the medium as imaginatively as anyone now writing. He paints pictures that would defy the literalism of cinema or TV. A man throwing himself off a bridge and landing on a barge-dog would probably cause complaints from the RSPCA if you showed it on TV but on radio you accept its grotesqueness. There's another scene in which a crane lowers an obelisk onto the octagonal tower of Blair's Gothic folly which is pure radio, though Blair's delight in the oddity of his construction ('I *do* like the mullioned window between the Doric columns – that has a quality of coy desperation, like a spinster gatecrashing a costume ball in a flowered frock . . . and the pyramid on the portico is sheer dumb insolence') reminds me of Alec Guinness's vicar rejoicing in his Chaucerian stained-glass in *Kind Hearts and Coronets*. Strangest of all is the scene where Mrs Blair is trying to put stitches into a neighing donkey in her drawing-room: instructed to let go of the donkey's legs and pick up a pair of forceps from the grate, Blair yells in agony because they are too hot, and gets kicked by the donkey at which point his collection of clocks starts furiously chiming. Stoppard delights in a mad, Mitfordesque world where the mundane, represented by the policeman Hogbin, has no place:

HOGBIN: I'm *terribly* sorry. I sat on your parrot.
MRS BLAIR: It's not as bad as it looks, he was already dead. Giles, do remove him. I've given up on lunch. I'm off to see Don Juan – he hasn't been getting his oats.

159

John Tydeman's Radio 3 production highlighted the tone of faintly privileged eccentricity through star-casting: Charles Gray as Blair with his chiselled Pall Mall voice, Penelope Keith at her imperious, fête-opening best as Mrs Blair, and Dinsdale Landen as the ideologically-confused Purvis. What Stoppard is saying in this blithely funny piece is that the English treat espionage as a superior chess game and have long lost sight of what the purpose of the game actually is, but that, as long as they go their madly capricious way, they are better off than those nations that believe in historical abstractions.

Squaring The Circle

Stoppard's understandable preoccupation with Eastern Europe gave us two fine plays in *Professional Foul* and *Every Good Boy Deserves Favour* and a clever, if ephemeral, one in *Dogg's Hamlet, Cahoot's Macbeth*. In *Squaring The Circle* he provides a TV drama–documentary about events in Poland between August 1980, when Solidarity launched its campaign for trade union rights, and December 1981 when martial law was declared under General Jaruzelski. As Stoppard makes clear in his pained and detailed preface, however, what appeared on British screens in May, 1984 was rather different from the 'dramatized personal essay' he had originally envisaged.

Drama-documentary always creates a problem. How do we know what is fact and what is speculation? Stoppard's original answer was two-fold: firstly, to put himself into the story as 'Author' interposing himself between us and recreated events to let us know what was fact and what was surmise; secondly, to offer us alternative versions of events at which no eye-witness could have been present. As a result of the intervention of the American company, Metromedia, who put 800,000 dollars into the financing of the film, Stoppard as 'Author' was replaced by the actor Richard Crenna as 'Narrator'. As Stoppard says, 'What was supposed to have been a kind of personal dramatized essay turned into a kind of play about an unexplained American in Poland.' After a good many battles, the alternative readings of crucial scenes stayed more or less intact. It is difficult to judge the finished result since it is not what Stoppard originally intended, but, as a script, *Squaring The Circle* is informative, interesting, definably Stoppardesque: it has the vitality of any

160

play dealing with momentous public events. My only doubt is about the need to remind us so constantly about authorial fallibility. A simple announcement at the start that the film was a reconstruction of recent events might have sufficed. Alternatively, like Robert Ardrey in his play about the Hungarian uprising *Shadow of Heroes*, Stoppard could simply have had the actors announce that they were 'speaking for' the characters they represent.

Having said that, the film does a number of valuable things. It puts the rise of Solidarity into the context of Polish history in one very good scene where the 'Narrator' and a 'Witness' sit in a café illustrating the dismemberment of Poland over the centuries by pushing bread-rolls around a table. It is an economical way of getting across the salient facts. It also reminds us how emigré Polish nationalists kept the idea of their country alive in the nineteenth century, how Poland repulsed Soviet Russia in 1920, how at Yalta Stalin was allowed to keep the prize of Poland and how, in 1970, the workers' revolts in the Baltic ports led to the killing of probably 200 people.

Stoppard also makes it clear in the film how the idea of Solidarity – much applauded in the West where that familiar blood-red symbol would appear on posters and car-stickers belonging to liberal and reactionary alike – was doomed because of a central, internal contradiction. Stoppard's Narrator spells it out clearly:

'Between August 1980 and December 1981 an attempt was made in Poland to put together two ideas which wouldn't fit, the idea of freedom as it is understood in the West and the idea of socialism as it is understood in the Soviet Empire. The attempt failed because it was impossible, in the same sense as it is impossible in geometry to turn a circle into a square with the same area – not because no-one has found out how to do it, but because there is no way in which it can be done.'

Stoppard, admittedly with the benefit of hindsight, understands something which the more optimistic commentators in the West didn't: that Solidarity's demands for the right to strike, freedom of expression, the broadcasting of Mass, economic reforms, medical, housing and welfare benefits would, if faithfully carried

161

through, have led to the gradual dismantling of the Communist state. Lech Walesa's radical opponent, Andrzej Gwiazda, gets it right when he says 'free trade unions are political'.

While Hugo Williams in the *New Statesman* thought that 'Stoppard's hero-worship of Walesa turns him into a cut-out', it seems to me that one of the good features of the film is that it shows there were strong elements of naïveté and vanity in Walesa's character. He ignores the prophetic warning of the intellectual Jacek Kuron that 'You can win little by little but remember if you lose you will lose overnight.' He fails to realise that you cannot limit and define a revolution and, in consequence, is virtually powerless to stop a wave of unauthorised strikes spreading across the country. He also rejoices in his celebrity though he has the shrewdness to cancel a visit to America where he would have become part of an anti-Communist carnival. Stoppard shows Walesa to be a brave and courageous man. He also shows, as the very title implies, that he was attempting the impossible.

Stoppard does two major things in this play. He dramatises recent history: a necessary process when the onrush of events often makes us forget how things started and evolved. He also reminds us of the fallibility of the supposedly omniscient commentator. Who knows what Brezhnev said to Gierek, First Secretary of the Polish Communist Party, when they met by the Black Sea in July 1980? Stoppard gives us two versions: one in which Brezhnev expresses his concern about events in Poland in the language of a *Pravda* editorial, another in which he shouts like a gangster 'What the hell is going on with you guys?' Again, who knows what happened at the tripartite meeting between Jaruzelski, Walesa and Archbishop Glemp on November 4, 1981? So Stoppard gives us three different versions. The first two are presented as card-games. In the first, Glemp attacks Walesa on the grounds that 'Socialism is order. Your extremists create disorder,' while Jaruzelski picks up the tricks. In the second, Glemp turns on Jaruzelski for reneging on the provisions of the Gdansk agreement. In the third, Glemp states a fundamental truth that 'without the economic problem there would be no political problem' and, indeed, one of the admirable things the play does is to remind us of Poland's steadily accumulating international debts and uncontrolled inflation. They partly explain the formation of Solidarity and the state's intransigence in the face of its demands.

Squaring The Circle is a tragedy in the guise of a quasi-documentary: by that I mean, it depicts the rise of an optimistic, spontaneous movement inexorably doomed to failure. It does so with a good deal of integrity, making no claims either to factual omniscience or moral superiority. It simply presents us with a situation where the Soviet Union's fear of breakaway movements and its practical need for a railway supply-line through to East Germany was bound eventually to lead to a military crackdown. Although this is Stoppard writing in one of his more sober and more self-restrained moods, it also is shot through with characteristically Stoppardian ideas. Kuron, the intellectual who attributes Walesa's failure to the lack of a 'reliable framework' is presented sympathetically. But at one point he passes through a playground where Walesa's children are playing and where they say that Mr Kuron thinks that if he leaves the Party alone, the Party will leave him alone. It is intended as a wounding criticism. The Witness (Stoppard's alter ego) calls that a cheap trick. But, *à propos* Kuron, he goes on: 'He's got it upside down in my opinion. Theories don't guarantee social justice, social justice tells you if a theory is any good. Right and wrong are not complicated – when a child cries 'That's not fair' the child can be believed. Children are always right.'

Just as in *Every Good Boy Deserves Favour* and *Professional Foul* Stoppard assumes that children have an instinctive, unforced, spontaneous moral sense which the State – with all its oppressive bureaucratic machinery – has somehow lost sight of.

Rough Crossing

George Axelrod once said that the big question about Neil Simon was whether he had a flop in him (it received a fairly decisive answer with *God's Favorite* in 1974). The same question might have been asked of Tom Stoppard. The answer came with *Rough Crossing*, a very free adaptation of Ferenc Molnar's *Play at the Castle*, which opened at the National Theatre on October 30, 1984 in a Peter Wood production. As with any resounding flop, one wondered how it ever got to be put on in the first place. Why should Stoppard devote so much energy to re-writing Molnar's light, pleasing comedy? And why should he insert into it a doggedly elaborate pastiche of a late

1920s Broadway musical? As Milton Shulman succinctly remarked: 'This play's major mistake is the assumption that it is possible to parody tripe.'

Molnar's elegant Hungarian comedy – which was translated by P.G. Wodehouse under the title *The Play's The Thing* and which achieved success on Broadway and in the West End – was about the interplay of reality and illusion. In a castle on the Italian Riviera a young composer is heartbroken at hearing his fiancée exchanging passionate sentiments with another man. In order to rescue the situation, Sandor Turai, a manipulative playwright translates life into art and dashes off a mock Sardou playlet incorporating the overhead dialogue. The young composer is persuaded that originally he simply eavesdropped on a rehearsal of the play. As shown in a revival at Greenwich Theatre in 1979, it is a delicate trifle in which there is a perfect proportion between means and ends.

What is startling about the Stoppard is its disruption of that harmony and the transformation of Molnar's playful artifice into leaden-footed parody. Stoppard translates the action to the SS *Italian Castle* sailing between Southampton and New York. Two middle-aged playwrights, Turai and Gal, and their composer-collaborator, Adam, are trying to find the perfect ending for their new Broadway musical comedy. Once again the composer is perturbed at hearing his fiancée, the actress Natasha, involved in a romantic escapade. To prevent the composer's premature disembarkation at Cherbourg, Turai writes this episode into the new musical which contains a plot of Byzantine complexity to do with jewel-thieves and white slave markets.

Stoppard's problem is that he does not so much paint the lily as tie gigantic bow ribbons around its stem. He turns Molnar's omniscient, Jeevesian footman, Dvornichek, into a land-based cabin-steward who obstinately refers to the ship's verandah as first balcony. He also adds a running gag in which the steward repeatedly misunderstands instructions and downs the Cognacs requested by Turai. The first couple of times the gag (similar to the old one on the radio programme ITMA in which Colonel Chinstrap purloined any passing drink with a cry of 'I don't mind if I do Sir') is quite funny but it stales with repetition. On top of that Stoppard endows the composer, Adam, with a speech-impediment that makes him answer questions that have been asked several seconds previously. Ayckbourn employed a similar joke in *The Norman Conquests* where Tom, the lugubrious vet, took a good thirty seconds to answer simple questions such as whether he would like a cup of coffee. That joke sprang from character and mental slowness: Stoppard's has a much more mechanical quality. He simply has Dvornichek and Turai ply Adam with questions and get him to answer the first rather than the second:

> TURAI: All unpacked? Found a place for everything?
> DVORNICHEK: I expect you'd like a drink, sir?
> ADAM: Oh yes, but I haven't brought much with me.
> DVORNICHEK: No problem, we've got plenty, you'll be all right with us.
> ADAM: No, I don't think I will.
> DVORNICHEK: Course you will – I trust your cabin is satisfactory?
> TURAI: How did you find your lady love?
> ADAM: Most comfortable, thank you.
> TURAI: Have you seen her yet?
> DVORNICHEK: Are you going to get one in?
> ADAM: Not yet, she's still at dinner.

The whole joke seems set up to lead to a mildly vulgar punch-line. Indeed what is most surprising about the play is the way Molnar's elegance of situation is turned into verbal by-play sometimes on a level not notably far above that of Little and Large or Cannon and Ball. When Adam says his muse is dead and that he will never write music again, Gal counters with: 'My dear boy, you're talking nonsense. I know about writer's block. What you need is the stewed prunes.' It is hard to credit that this is really Tom Stoppard.

What in the end sinks the play is the second act shipboard run-through of the putative Broadway musical. It is hard here to see exactly what Stoppard is parodying. In the late 20s and early 30s it was quite fashionable to set musicals on board ship – Cole Porter's *Anything Goes* is the most famous example – and even to interweave high society and low thievery. But Stoppard comes up with an inextricably complex plot that is miles away from the essential boy-meets-girl fable of the time, that is so preposterous it suggests the Turai–Gal–Adam show is a clinker from the start and that also takes us a long way from the play's starting-point which is the need to reassure Adam of his fiancée's fidelity by reconstructing the overheard love-scene. In the theatre, there seemed something crushingly heavy about the whole enterprise: when you have to get laughs in the second act by showing the leaning-tower in the so-called Pisa Room shooting up straight your show is in trouble. Stoppard says he likes doing adaptations because he doesn't have continual ideas for new plays. But there seems something extravagantly pointless about taking a perfectly good play, adapting it freely and making it less effective than it was before. If the Molnar is any good, why not play it as it is? If not, why bother with it in the first place?

Dalliance

Stoppard's penchant for adaptation continued with this version of Schnitzler's *Liebelei*: a play that was a huge success at the Vienna Burgtheater in 1895, its truthful portrayal of the consequences of casual masculine pleasure-seeking causing something of a storm. Stoppard's version opened at the National Theatre on May 28, 1986 and raised a large number of questions about the propriety of fiddling around with Schnitzler's original text and decorating his language with Stoppardisms, and also about the morality of transposing the last act to back-stage at the Josefstadt theatre where a schmaltzy Viennese operetta is noisily in rehearsal. Stoppard is such a good and intelligent writer that one wishes he could find better employment than in these parasitic re-writes of other men's work.

For two of its three acts, Stoppard's version adheres with reasonable fidelity to the original. We see Christine – the *susse Mädel* or working-class sweet-girl of Viennese society – romantically attached to Fritz, a medical student and part-time dragoon who is heavily embroiled in an affair with a married woman. Christine's more hard-headed friend, Mizi, also becomes involved with Fritz's friend, Theodore. To the men, the girls are just a couple of 'popsies'. But while Fritz plays the game of love according to Vienna rules, Christine is deeply smitten and ignorant of the fact that Fritz has been challenged to a duel by his mistress's husband.

Even while observing the line of Schnitzler's plot, Stoppard cannot resist adding jokes in a style far removed from the original. When Mizi announces that she is a seamstress at the theatre, Theodore limply responds: 'Seams, madam, I know not seams.' And when, in a first-act dinner party, Theodore acts up the role of a *sommelier*, he cries: 'You'll find this an affectionate little wine with just a hint of promiscuity.' That kind of joke stems from Thurber, not Schnitzler and sits up and begs attention in a way that is inappropriate.

It is in the third act that Stoppard most drastically cuts loose from Schnitzler's play. In the original it is set in Christine's modest, neat room in the humble apartment she shares with her father. She learns the truth about Fritz's death in a duel, awakens to the cruel realisation that for him she was just a pastime and goes off to his grave and her own almost certain death while her pit-violinist father sinks to the floor sobbing crying 'She won't come back – she won't come back.' The force of the emotion in that humble setting can – as the Vienna Burgtheater production which came to London in 1973 showed – be overwhelming. Stoppard, however, translates the action to backstage at the Josefstadt theatre where a travesty dragoon and his travesty inamorata are rehearsing a Strauss number about a false hussar. Thus the reality of Christine's passion is counter-pointed by the theatrical artifice of the love being sung about onstage. Stoppard also makes Christine more vehement in her denunciation of Theodore ('You shitbucket', she here calls him) while denying her the final hint of suicide.

The pain and honesty of Schnitzler's play survives; and Brenda Blethyn's peformance as Christine at the National was toweringly good. As Benedict Nightingale said: 'What's admirable about Blethyn's performance is that not merely does she refuse to sentimentalise or romanticise Christine, she fully admits she's gauche, awkward, abjectly possessive and, because of that possessiveness, increasingly unattractive.' But it is surprising that a dramatist of Stoppard's integrity – one so worried about the confusion of fact and fiction in a play like *Squaring The Circle* – is so seemingly cavalier in his treatment of another dramatist's play. Do we not have a responsibility to dead writers as well as living ones? If Schnitzler deliberately set the last two acts in Christine's frugal and modest room was that not for an artistic purpose? If his style is one of dignified sobriety, is it not a bit odd to trick it out with Stoppardian puns?

Stoppard has not destroyed the original play as in *Rough Crossing*. But he has added his own 'improvements' in a manner that is artistically questionable. I am left feeling that Stoppard – a writer of wit, originality, ingenuity and, latterly, powerful moral and political conviction – should be giving us his own works rather than exhuming and re-siting other people's. What we crave from Stoppard is another new play of his own.

6

Stoppard in Context

In a book like this, one tends to write about Stoppard in isolation from the other dramatists around him. But, as a critic, I am well aware that he is simply a part of a very varied theatrical landscape: that Stoppard's cerebral wit, philosophical inquiry and latter-day political conviction are balanced by Ayckbourn's painful comedy, Nichols's displays of ravaged feeling, Bond's positive hatred of existing society, Shaffer's spectacular theatricality, Hare's sharp attacks on post-war failure and personal corruption. All good dramatists stake out territory that is peculiarly their own. Just as the epithet Pinteresque has come to mean a domestic power-game implicit with threat so the adjective 'Stoppardian' would signify to most people a well-shaped theatrical extravaganza filled with conflicting arguments and a plethora of jokes.

I am struck, however, by the marked difference in tone and style between Stoppard's work and that of many of his con-temporaries. He, in effect, was launched into British theatre in 1967 with *Rosencrantz and Guildenstern Are Dead*. In one sense, the play fed off the anti-romantic view of *Hamlet* established by Peter Hall at Stratford in 1965, and a European tradition of drama, spearheaded by Beckett, that saw life as apparently without meaning or purpose. But Stoppard, an apolitical relativist, came into British theatre at a time when dramatists were becoming increasingly certain in their political attitudes, critical of their environment and even didactic in their methods. As Cathy Itzen has written, 'the significant British theatre of 1968-78 was primarily theatre of political change.' The fascination of the young with radical politics throughout the world; the growth to maturity of a generation that had benefited from the 1945 Butler Education act; the speed of communica-tion; the disappointment in Britain with the slowness of changes instituted by the Wilson Labour Government; and, in theatrical terms, the abolition of the Lord Chamberlain's powers of censorship and the sudden growth of small, experimental, unofficial theatres all over London – all these made the late 60s in Britain a period of extraordinary artistic ferment. In one sense, Stoppard participated, embracing the possibilities afforded by Ed Berman's Inter-Action in Soho, but, in another, he was separate from a movement that began to judge drama in terms of its social efficacy. In *Stages in the Revolution* Ms Itzin lists 43 plays produced in 1968 that were in the broadest sense 'political'. You can't imagine Stoppard feeling he had much in common with the Bond of *Early Morning* or the John McGrath of *Bakke's Night of Fame* let alone *The Agitprop Street Players* and *Rent's Play*.

It is not merely that Stoppard was different from his contemporaries in his lack of political certainty. He was also very different in his choice of themes. He wrote about attendant lords at Elsinore, theatre critics, a Boswellian historian, a moral philosopher with a disintegrating wife at a time when other dramatists were more concerned with the state of the nation than of individual souls. Peter Barnes' *The Ruling Class* in 1968 was an exuberant Gothic fantasy but also a play about an England in which, as the title implies, there was a governing class ruled by madness and grotesquerie. Peter Nichols's *The National Health* in 1969 brilliantly used a hospital ward in a decaying Victorian edifice as a microcosm for a society in which the individual was doing battle against organisation. John Osborne in *West of Suez* in 1971 went further still and came up with a remarkable play (echoing both *Heartbreak House* and *The Cherry Orchard*) about a culture in decline, about over-civilised people hiding behind ironical defences and about a brutal new world waiting to take them over: 'My god, they've shot the fox' was the resonant final line implying the new barbarism about to take over from a tired, lassitudinous ruling class. Another writer, with a similarly elegiac quality, had three years previously written an exuberant revue about twentieth-century England: Alan Bennett's *40 Years On*. Like Osborne, Bennett saw the absurdity, the snobbery, the class-ridden vanity of the England that was in decline; but, again like Osborne, he saw the sadness as well as the historical necessity of its departure. When I first became a full-time drama critic in 1971 the state-of-England play was rapidly becoming the commonest theatrical form.

Stoppard seemed to belong in a different, more European tradition whose ancestors were Beckett, Kafka, Ionesco. He also wrote English with the fantastic ingenuity of someone like Nabokov who saw words as brilliant manipulative counters.

Stoppard's isolation from the dramatists around him intensified in the early 1970s, years which saw the rise of a whole new generation of maverick talents disgusted by the shoddy, materialist, corrupt spectacle of British public life and united in their belief that they should do something about it. Drama, in their hands, became not so much a means of initiating change as of registering protest: raising two disdainful fingers at the Britain they had grown up in. 1972 saw Stoppard's *Jumpers* installed at the Old Vic and *Artist Descending a Staircase* broadcast on radio. It was also the year of David Hare's *The Great Exhibition* which took as its hero a Labour MP given to growing pot and flashing at night in the park. What was remarkable was Mr Hare's comprehensive, Osborne-like list of targets which included parliamentary democracy, middle-class despair, unfeeling upper-class arrogance, fake hippiedom, Ibsenite drama, avant-garde posturing and George Orwell: it was a wild, flailing play spiced with Mr Hare's bilious wit. While that was playing at Hampstead Theatre Trevor Griffiths was confirming the promise he had shown in *Occupations* with *Sam Sam* at the Open Space. This was a lacerating play about two brothers: an unemployed, under-educated one swamped by Admass tat and dimly aware of a world elsewhere, and a working-class fugitive who had graduated to a milieu of chic radicalism and was desperately miserable. Mr Griffiths seemed to be saying that if you're born into a working-class background you're bound to be exploited: either by a stifling social system or by a class bred to exercise mastery in personal relationships.

1972 (how rich it seems in retrospect) also brought us Caryl Churchill's *Owners* which put the finger on a voracious female property-developer who gobbles up everything in sight and who turns the screw on a pair of working-class tenants blocking the sale of her property: she even takes over the wife's baby as part of her incessant acquisitiveness. What was heartening was that it was drama of the kind still pretty rare at that time in Britain: one that related private passions to public issues. Public events were tackled even more directly in the multi-authored *England's Ireland* (contributors included Howard Brenton, Brian Clark,

David Edgar, David Hare and Snoo Wilson) which argued that the Irish crisis had to be seen in the context of a long-standing social injustice as well as religious bigotry. It accused all British political parties of a criminally negligent attitude towards Ulster before the eruption of violence and asked how one could hope for a return to normal when 'normality' meant an unemployment rate in some areas of 43 per cent, a weekly wage of £11 and an overall situation in which 5 per cent of the population owned 47 per cent of the wealth. It argued, sanely, that the only hope for Ulster lay in political negotiation rather than in a renewed attempt to meet violence with violence. British drama suddenly seemed wide open to the discussion of the most immediate social and political issues: durability, finesse, the classic rules of good playwriting were of less importance than nailing the hypocrisy, mendacity and sheer nastiness that many young dramatists saw seeping through public life. It was even possible to attack public figures: Howard Barker's *Alpha Alpha* at the Open Space was about two readily-identifiable criminal brothers from the East End and about the radical chic of an ermine-caped peer who offered them his protection so long as they improved his visiting list. The play was a wonderfully virulent attack on the sentimentality and sadism often found in the criminal fraternity and on the opportunism of those who exploit murderous hoods for their own social and sexual advantage.

The whirligig of time brings in its revenges. Stoppard's *Jumpers* is periodically revived: most of the other plays from 1972 gather dust on the shelves or are forgotten. That's partly because it's a consciously-shaped work of art, partly because it deals with timeless issues. But drama can be journalistic as well as eternal, can tap a mood, draw attention to an issue, heighten awareness as well as deal with permanent truths. Shaw once said of *A Doll's House* that it will be forgotten when *A Midsummer Night's Dream* is still being played but that 'it will have done more work in the world.' He was wrong in that Ibsen's play is part of the permanent repertoire: he was right in that plays can legitimately have an immediate, political effect. The often raw, angry plays of the early 1970s were necessary at a time when Tory values were being re-asserted and when Britain was still in a period of long, post-imperial decline. I don't value the early work of Hare, Griffiths, Churchill, Barker any less than that of Stoppard simply because it seems to have fulfilled its immediate purpose. The failure to revive any of it may also be as much a comment on our Kleenex-theatre as on any inherent flaws in the work itself (though it was interesting to note that Howard Barker's *Claw* was revived by Theatre Clwyd ten years after its première).

Stoppard himself, an intelligent and self-critical writer, was obviously aware of the distance between himself and many of his fellow-practitioners. He spoke about it in many interviews. One of the most detailed and revealing was published in *Theatre Quarterly* in the May-July 1974 issue. The Editors questioned his views on the presumed impotence of political art and suggested his plays tend to bear on life in an oblique, distant, generalised way. Stoppard's reply:

'Well that's what art is best at. The objective is the universal perception, isn't it? By all means realize that perception in terms of a specific event, even a specific political event, but I'm not impressed by art *because* it's political. I believe in art being good or bad art, not relevant art or irrelevant art. The plain truth is that if you are angered or disgusted by a particular injustice or immorality, and you want to do something about it, *now, at once*, then you can hardly do worse than write a play about it. That's what art is bad at. But the less plain truth is that *without* that play and plays like it, without artists, the injustice will *never* be eradicated. In other words, because of Athol Fugard, to stretch a point.'

That's fair and sees both sides of the argument: that good politics doesn't make for good writing but that you cannot eliminate politics from the arena of art. Where I disagree with Stoppard is in his assumption that 'good' and 'bad' are inherently more important than 'relevant' or 'irrelevant' as critical adjectives. I sit through a lot of plays: I would rather watch an artistically-flawed play about an important subject than a piece of Swiss-clock precision-making about nothing very much. Examples will prove my point. David Edgar's *Maydays* was a large, sprawling, somewhat diffuse play about the failure of the dreams and desires of the revolutionary Sixties and Seventies: about political, personal, social failure. It was a relevant play that reached beyond the confines of the Barbican Theatre where it was presented and touched off debate in the columns of the newspapers. Simon Gray's *The Common*

Pursuit was a witty, ironic, well-honed play about, in the author's own words, 'English, middle-class, Cambridge-educated friendship.' It led to a very amusing diary of the production by Mr Gray himself but, although well-written, it was a play that never seemed to connect with a large public. Mr Gray's play may, by Stoppardian canons, be classified as good art. But the failures and disappointments of a group of literary careerists are of less interest (to me anyway) than the compromises and retreats of those who once believed that Britain was capable of profound social change.

Stoppard says he does not believe in art being relevant or irrelevant but good or bad. If you extend that argument logically, *Move Over Mrs Markham* (a first-rate Cooney-Chapman farce) seems inherently superior to, say, David Hare's *Plenty*, which deals ambitiously but not totally successfully with the collapse of post-war dreams and the inability of its heroine to find a place for herself in English society. One does not simply ask of a play if it is good of its kind. One has to ask if the kind itself is worth pursuing. Also plays do not exist in some kind of aesthetic vacuum where they can be marked on a scale from 1 to 100. They exist in a particular moment at a particular time. Athol Fugard is a very good example of what I mean. *Sizwe Bansi is Dead* or *Statements After An Arrest Under the Immorality Act* were not death-defying masterpieces. But they were very necessary plays and seeing them in London at the Royal Court in 1974 helped to bring home to a lot of us in a very tangible way the appalling and evil consequences of apartheid. The irony is that Fugard's more immediately topical plays – performed by actors like John Kani and Winston Ntshona – have had a tremendous impact around the world. It is only when Fugard tries to write Ibsenite works of art – such as *A Taste of Aloes* or *The Road To Mecca* – that he falls prey to heavy-handed symbolism and the clanking machinery of old-fashioned plot devices.

Stoppard writes the kind of plays that suit him best. But it is wrong to draw from that general conclusions about the supposed impotence of political art. Drama is a mansion with an almost infinite number of rooms: I see no point in shutting off any of them. Instead of talking about the impotence of political art, it might be more relevant to talk of its inevitability. You cannot stop dramatists wanting to use the theatre as a platform for their views or as a means of responding to the society around them. What is significant is how different Stoppard is in style and tone from most of his contemporaries. In 1974, *Travesties* questioned the fallibility of memory, used a famous historical coincidence as a source of fun and debunked Marxism while equating Leninism with Fascism as a form of totalitarianism.

Other dramatists in 1974 used historical figures in just as free and easy a way as Stoppard but to vastly different effect. Howard Brenton's *The Churchill Play*, which had its première at Nottingham Playhouse, was actually set in 1984 when England had become a country of concentration camps. But its main political thrust came from a play presented by the internees to a Parliamentary delegation amounting to a ferocious attack on Winston Churchill. It is generally assumed that in May 1940 England found in Churchill a man who could save her. As Harold Hobson wrote of the Nottingham production: 'The haunting and alarming suggestion made in Mr Brenton's powerful play is that the man England found was the wrong man; that the war of 1939-45 was less Hitler's war than Churchill's; that the British, and especially the Scottish, people were so demoralised by bombing that they bitterly resented Churchill's keeping them at war; and that this was the cause of loss of empire and the moment when our freedom went.' Brenton's play could hardly be further from Stoppard's in its political views. It actually seems no less remarkable in the vigour of its imagination (it begins sensationally with Churchill rising from his coffin) or the mystery of its poetry. In the end, it even seems a more important play (more 'relevant' if you wish) in that it sees Churchill as the enemy of the people and the architect of our misfortunes as much as the saviour of our nation. I am not arguing that Brenton is right: merely that he raises profound and important issues (derived from Angus Calder's *The People's War*) about British society.

Like Stoppard, Peter Barnes is a dramatist who believes that seriousness and frivolity can be mixed; and his play *The Bewitched* (which played alongside *Travesties* in the Aldwych repertory in 1974) combined Jonsonian invective with musical comedy and vaudeville. Where it differed profoundly from Stoppard was in its vision of authority. The play took a jocular, ironic look at Carlos II, the last male heir of the Spanish Hapsburgs, who was a slack-jawed, incontinent, epileptic, impotent physical wreck. What Mr Barnes noisily satirised was the absurdity of swathing such a sad, hapless figure in the trappings of divinely-appointed power. By implication, he questioned all authority, all divisions of society into shearers and shorn, all attempts to place one human being in authority over another. It seemed at the time a rambling, overwritten play, though it would be good to have a second chance to judge it, but it could hardly have been further from Stoppard in its hatred of hierarchies and its contempt for the notion of monarchical power.

Surprisingly, perhaps, the dramatist who came closest to Stoppard in using historical figures to exemplify the ultimate political impotence of art was Edward Bond, whose play about Shakespeare, *Bingo*, arrived at the Royal Court in 1974 after being seen earlier at the Northcott Theatre, Exeter. The governing theme of the play is the luxury of creativity in a world full of institutionalised violence (which takes us back to Henry Carr's remark that 'To be an artist *at all* is like living in Switzerland during a world war'). We see Shakespeare in the last year of his life at New Place, Stratford, sitting pensively in his garden while local smallholders are ruined and common land enclosed, cutting himself off from the almost Strindbergian terrors of the dark house and the detested wife, and brooding on the cruelty of his age with its executions, its prisons, its public floggings and its barbaric sports. 'They were hanged and whipped so I could be free,' he says of society's victims; and, as he finally kills himself, he constantly cries 'Was anything done?' as if his whole life had been a failure to come to terms with the encircling evil. As Harold Hobson (the most truly perceptive of modern critics) wrote at the time: 'Men are killed; women vagrants are hanged; bears are most cruelly baited. Bond's Shakespeare feels at all this repulsion and pity. But what has he actually done to stop it? He has concluded a profitable property deal with his friend Mr Combe (the agreement still exists) and written a few plays. It is not in his opinion enough.'

While Bond chafes and rages at the insufficiency of art to change society, Stoppard happily accepts it. And while Bond in *Bingo* works on the emotions, Stoppard in *Travesties* appeals primarily to the intellect. There is a terrifying climax in *Bingo* where Shakespeare's hated wife and daughter beat fearsomely on the locked door of his bedroom while he agonisingly dies: terrifying because it shows Shakespeare's failure in the simplest of tasks which is to love and be loved by his surrounding family.

That, in the end, I believe has more to do with real drama than writing a scene (as Stoppard does in *Travesties*) in which Joyce's quizzing of Tzara is simultaneously an echo of Lady Bracknell interrogating Jack Worthing, a replay of the eighth chapter of *Ulysses* and a potted history of Dada. Stoppard is a dramatist of tremendous intellectual brilliance. But sometimes in the theatre the most potent effects are the simplest.

1977 was the year Stoppard came out. In *Every Good Boy Deserves Favour* and *Professional Foul* he nailed his colours to the mast and attacked the Soviet violation of human rights and the philosophical belief that right and wrong are verbal rather than instinctual concepts. I have argued earlier that Stoppard's concern and commitment gave him new strength as a writer and even rescued him from the gadfly dazzle that was rapidly becoming his trademark. He began to accept the dramatist's need to make a personal statement. But it is fascinating to compare the work of Stoppard, the emigré Czech and recent visitor to the Soviet Union, with that of Alan Bennett who also happened in 1977 to produce a play set in the Soviet Union, *The Old Country*. Stoppard in *Every Good Boy* sees that vast country as one unable to tolerate freedom of thought but embarrassed by its reflex persecution of individuals and craving acceptance in the West: Bennett uses the Soviet Union as an opportunity both to satirise and debate the nature of Englishness.

Bennett's play is cunning and artful. It begins with a country house; wine, talk, friends; Elgar on the turntable and light irony round the drinks table. Only gradually do we realise that it is set not in Ruislip but in the spruce-backed Russian dacha of a Foreign-Office defector undergoing a visit from his sister and pillar-of-the-British-Establishment brother-in-law. What follows is a complex study of England. Hilary, the hero, may have defected thirteen years ago and be working as a translator in Moscow but he still lapses into *Times* obituary notices and Buchanesque adventures and keeps people at bay with the English irony that is both a defence and a delight. What tension the play generates springs from his brother-in-law's request that he return home. But Bennett's point is that he has never really left it: that, at a certain level of class and accomplishment, the English never shake off a love of books and countryside, a deadly detachment and a sense of being emotionally wounded. Home, in short, is where the hurt is.

Bennett writes like a poet: elegiac, melancholic, parodistic. He has a capacity to satirise the Englishness he loves that Stoppard cannot aspire to. What Stoppard has – especially in his later works – is the ability to see that the middle-class Englishness he himself adores exists in a context of East European repression (one might add South African and South American as well but Stoppard has not got round to those). *Every Good Boy* and *Professional Foul* remind us forcibly that our cherished Western freedoms are not to be taken lightly and that others are punished for presuming to the rights that we unthinkingly enjoy. There is a line in *The Old Country* where the tribulations of Solzhenitsyn are shrugged off with 'Which is worse – five years in a camp or three pages in *The Listener*?' I don't suggest for a moment that is Alan Bennett's view, but the parochialism that lies behind that line is something you would emphatically not find in Stoppard. And, deeply enjoyable as *The Old Country* is, it still manages to ignore the realities of Soviet life in order to study the English temper. Stoppard may be bourgeois-English; but he is also, as his later works emphasise, a citizen of the wider world.

Stoppard's progress in the last ten years has, in fact, been a matter of some frustration to those of us who welcome his increasingly political involvement. He has, as I have indicated, advanced to the point where he is both unashamed to state a point of view and capable of writing about common human passions with eloquence and emotion. *Professional Foul* and *The Real Thing* are both major achievements. My regret is that he spends so much time on adaptations which are not invariably successful and which seem like a diversion from his true task (he has also co-written a film *Brazil* and translated the libretto of *The Love of Three Oranges*).

He has, of course, explained on many occasions that he is not good on plots and that ideas for plays don't exactly leap unbidden to mind. But my fear is that the relative slowness of Stoppard's original output in the last few years is a symptom of the declining state of theatre in Britain. It is surprising how rarely our best dramatists do actually now write plays. Harold Pinter devotes much of his energy to directing. Peter Shaffer spends much of his time nursing and nurturing the hit-play he writes every five or six years. Trevor Griffiths devotes much of his time to films and television where he sees real possibilities of affecting society. Michael Frayn is diversifying into films. Alan Bennett likewise seems to prefer screens large and small. Peter Nichols, David Storey, John Osborne seem to be retreating towards autobiography and fiction. We have in Britain an almost unparalleled range of dramatists. The only one who consistently writes at least one play every year (helped by the fact he runs his own theatre) is Alan Ayckbourn. But, on the whole, there is a gradual drift away from theatre towards movies, television and the more private consolations of the hardback book. New young writers, of course, appear all the time. But I have the feeling that British theatre – penurious, struggling and lacking the kind of natural constituency it has enjoyed for two decades – no longer exists at the centre of our culture and exerts the attraction for writers it once did.

There are many reasons for this. The thinness of subsidy in the public sector; the dearth of enterprising producers (Michael Codron and Robert Fox are two of the few) in the commercial sector; the heavy reliance on a tourist audience to keep our theatre alive. British theatre no longer seems to address itself to a coherent group but to a motley community made up of hardcore local theatregoers who endeavour to see everything, of occasional punters looking for a night out and of armies of Americans drawn to Britain partly by the promise of a culture much healthier than the one they find back home. British theatre is heading all the time towards blandness, safety and caution.

That is why, as a critic, I crave new work from Tom Stoppard because, whatever he is, he is not safe or bland. At the time of writing his latest work for the theatre is a faithful adaptation of a play by the Czech writer, Vaclav Havel, presented by the Bristol Old Vic (in October, 1986). Verbally elegant and ironically repetitive, the play may seem in some ways like an expression of a highly Stoppardian viewpoint. Its hero is a moral philosopher in an unnamed totalitarian state. Having offended the authorities, he seeks a life of privacy and seclusion. But he is visited first by two fans from a papermill who want him to become a literary figurehead and who leave him stacks of paper with which to make his statement of protest. He is then visited by two state policemen who want him to sign a document denying authorship of the original, offending article. Either by prosecuting a cause he no longer totally believes in or by denying past authorship, he invalidates himself. And his final, despairing cry is a heartfelt one of 'Leave me alone.'

Havel's play is clearly an eloquent statement of his own predicament as a writer persecuted and imprisoned by the Czech authorities; and his plea for individual privacy might, at one stage, have coincided with Stoppard's own sentiments. But what is fascinating about Stoppard is that he has gradually moved from stylish, apolitical disengagement towards an active involvement with current issues in works like *Every Good Boy Deserves Favour*, *Professional Foul*, *Night and Day*, *Dogg's Hamlet, Cahoot's Macbeth*, *The Real Thing*, *The Dog It Was That Died* and *Squaring the Circle*. I believe this has made him a richer, better writer in that his wit, intelligence and ingenuity are now enlisted on the side of the preservation of basic freedoms, a profound hatred of tyranny and a belief in the dignity of the individual. Stoppard is still an entertainer; but he is an entertainer with a definable ideal.

I began this book by saying that I viewed Stoppard's career with 'pleasurable bewilderment'. The bewilderment stemmed largely from his denial of art's basic importance and from the faintly dehumanised, abstract quality of some of his early work. I still feel that. But, in the end, the pleasure greatly outweighs the bewilderment because Stoppard has shown that he can write about moral and political issues with buzzing eloquence, because he has taught himself to write about real people with passionate ingenuity and because he has written about serious matters with light-spirited gravity. His work is now anchored in steadfast belief and a communicated delight in character. At a time when I believe drama, on the pendulum-swing theory, is slowly heading back towards greater audience involvement and emotional identification with the people on stage, it will be fascinating to see whether Stoppard goes with the trend or bucks it. Whatever he does, the words 'a new Stoppard' will continue to send a quiver of anticipation down my back.

Bibliography

Works by Tom Stoppard:

Lord Malquist and Mr Moon (Faber 1966)
Rosencrantz and Guildenstern are Dead (Faber 1967)
Enter A Free Man (Faber 1968)
The Real Inspector Hound (Faber 1968)
Albert's Bridge and *If You're Glad I'll Be Frank*
    (Faber 1969)
After Magritte (Faber 1971)
Jumpers (Faber 1972)
Artist Descending a Staircase and *Where Are They Now?*
    (Faber 1973)
Travesties (Faber 1975)
Dirty Linen and New-Found-Land (Faber 1976)
Night and Day (Faber 1978)
Every Good Boy Deserves Favour and *Professional Foul*
    (Faber 1978)
Dogg's Hamlet, Cahoot's Macbeth (Faber 1980)
Undiscovered Country (Faber 1980)
On The Razzle (Faber 1981)
The Dog It Was That Died and Other Plays (Faber 1983)
Squaring The Circle (Faber 1984)
The Real Thing (Faber 1982)
Four Plays For Radio (Faber 1984)
Rough Crossing (Faber 1985)

Other books consulted:

File on Stoppard Compiled by Malcolm Page
    (Methuen 1986)
Dada and Surrealism by Dawn Ades
    (Thames and Hudson 1974)

Post-War British Theatre Criticism by John Elsom
(Routledge and Kegan Paul 1981)
The Theatre of the Absurd by Martin Esslin
(Penguin Books 1961)
Tom Stoppard by Ronald Hayman
(Heinemann Educational Books 1977)
Stages in the Revolution by Catherine Itzin
(Eyre Methuen 1980)
An Introduction to 50 Modern British Plays
by Benedict Nightingale (Pan Books 1982)
A Concise History of Modern Painting by Herbert Read
(Prager 1975)
Show People by Kenneth Tynan
(Weidenfeld and Nicolson 1980)
Plays, Prose Writing and Poems by Oscar Wilde
(Everyman 1967)
The Fontana Dictionary of Modern Thought Edited by
Alan Bullock and Oliver Stallybrass
(Fontana/Collins 1977)

Index